Child Care:
Emerging Legal Issues

The *Journal of Children in Contemporary Society* series:

Child Care:
Emerging Legal Issues

Edited by
Mary Frank, MS in Education

The Haworth Press
New York

Child Care: Emerging Legal Issues has also been published as *Journal of Children in Contemporary Society,* Volume 15, Number 4, Summer 1983.

The Haworth Press, Inc., 28 East 22 Street, New York, NY 10010

Library of Congress Cataloging in Publication Data
Main entry under title:

Child care.

    Also published as Journal of children in contemporary society; v. 15, no. 4 (Summer 1983)
    Bibliography: p.
    1. Children—Legal status, laws, etc.—United States—Addresses, essays, lectures.
I. Frank, Mary (Mary Isabelle) II. Series.
KF479.A75C47 1983   344.73'0327   83-12929
ISBN 0-86656-182-X   347.304327

Child Care:
Emerging Legal Issues

Journal of Children in Contemporary Society
Volume 15, Number 4

CONTENTS

WELFARE ISSUES

CHILD ADVOCACY

MARSHA POSTER ROSENBLOOM, *Director, Carnegie-Mellon University Child Care Center, Pittsburgh*
JUDITH RUBIN, ATR, *Western Psychiatric Institute & Clinic, Pittsburgh*
ETHEL M. TITTNICH, *Adjunct Assistant Professor, Program of Child Development and Child Care, School of Health Related Professions, University of Pittsburgh*

Child Care:
Emerging Legal Issues

Introduction

> The law is the last result of human wisdom acting upon human experience for the benefit of the Public. *Samuel Johnson*

New Federalism and Block Grants are terms that have become "household words." Familiar as this terminology is to legislators, to professionals, and to others, there still exists a fragmented understanding of the legislative changes that encompass it. The intent of this issue is to develop a body of knowledge that identifies these changes in a unified fashion so that readers may possibly use this understanding to advocate for more responsive legislation. The term "Child Care" in the theme title is used to reflect society's responsibility toward the care of its children. It is *not* to be interpreted as the daily care provided by day care agencies. The term "Emerging Legal Issues" is used to identify the child-related legislative changes that have been initiated at the federal level over the last several years.

To clarify and simplify the complexities inherent in the legislative changes, the content is designed to focus on the changes as they occur within the federal health, education, and welfare programs and how they impact on state and local practice. Within each section, the contributors have developed an introduction that provides background information for an understanding of the present policy; they have developed an in-depth study on the new policies; and they have identified several existing models designed to implement the new program.

Underlying these changes at the federal level are the concerns of the child advocates at the local level. For approximately the past fifteen years, those in the child care and related professions have become aware of the need to develop a knowledge base that would enable them to influence public policy on behalf of children. So far, their efforts have been somewhat successful, but there is a need to further expand their skills. At the conclusion of this issue, there are two articles on child advocacy. One is written by a lawyer and one is written by a professor of child development. Within these two articles are new understandings and new strategies that can serve all child advocates who wish to be highly instrumental in bringing about needed public policy changes.

This comprehensive compendium of articles was brought together by those who have dedicated their efforts toward the advancement of children in our society. We are grateful to Bob Horowitz who has capably functioned as the theme consultant and as a contributor. We are deeply appreciative to all the contributors who have earnestly put forth their best efforts to translate complex issues into an understandable framework of reference. Individually, all the contributors are nationally recognized for their expertise within their own field. We are grateful also, to Carla Frank for the graphics within this issue.

MIF

Introduction

Sara Rosenbaum, JD

In 1935, as part of the Social Security Act, Congress created the Maternal and Child Health and Crippled Children's programs[1] in order to provide formula grants to states to promote health care for disadvantaged mothers and children. Since that modest beginning nearly 50 years ago,[2] the federal commitment to improving health care for disadvantaged children and mothers has grown dramatically, as federal policymakers have increasingly come to realize that the availability, distribution and accessibility of adequate health care for the poor is a matter of national concern. This commitment has yielded profound results in terms of both increased access to health care by poor Americans, and improvements in their health status.[3] (See Table 1).

After almost a half century of growth and progress in federal maternal and child health programs, however, the Reagan Administration has sought to lessen this commitment, utilizing the major tools available to the Executive Branch: a sweeping legislative agenda, major regulatory revisions, and relaxation of enforcement machinery. During the Administration's first two years, Congress rejected certain specific Administration's proposals and even made some positive structural improvements in federal health programs. The Administration has succeeded, however, in severely damaging federal health programs for children by reducing federal expen-

Sara Rosenbaum is Senior Health Specialist, Children's Defense Fund, 1520 New Hampshire Avenue, N.W., Washington, D.C. 20036.

3

TABLE 1. Federal/State Health Programs

SOCIAL SECURITY ACT TITLE V: Maternal & Child Health (MCH) Crippled Childrens Services (CCS) Program of Projects: Maternal/Infant Care Children & Youth Dental Health Neonatal Intensive Care Family Planning Supplementary Security Income Research/Demonstration	SOCIAL SECURITY ACT TITLE XIX: Medicaid Program for Poor Women & Children Early Periodic Screening Diagnosis & Treatment (EPSDT)
	PUBLIC HEALTH SERVICE ACT TITLE X: Family Planning Programs
SOCIAL SECURITY ACT TITLE XX: Family Planning Services Aid to Families with Dependent Children (AFDC)	PUBLIC HEALTH SERVICE ACT SECTION 330 Community Health Centers
	SPECIAL SUPPLEMENTAL FOOD PROGRAM FOR WOMEN, INFANTS & CHILDREN (WIC)

ditures by billions of dollars at the very time when recession and unemployment have combined to dramatically swell the ranks of impoverished and uninsured families dependent on the public health system.

The major victims of this dramatic redirection of federal policy are 12.3 million children[4] living below the federal poverty level. They represent 19.8% of all children in the nation and their numbers have increased by nearly a million during the past year.[5] The disadvantages from which these children suffer are graphically revealed by significantly greater rates of illness, disability, morbidity and mortality than their wealthier counterparts.[6] This has been especially true for minority infants and children who, even in 1980, were three times as likely to have a mother who died in childbirth and twice as likely to die during the first year of life.[7]

Despite substantial progress over the past 50 years, as of 1980, poor children's unmet health needs continued to represent a significant national social problem. Without regard to their continued pressing problems, or to the considerable body of data demonstrating the need for ongoing federal intervention,[8] however, the Reagan Administration has undertaken a major effort to undermine, defund and repeal effective federal maternal and child health programs.

It should be noted at the outset that the multi-faceted effort by the Administration to refashion federal maternal and child health policy is not a phenomenon unique to health. Indeed, the Administration is employing similar approaches in other domestic program areas where comprehensive federal policy and enforcement schemes have developed, such as education, nutrition, housing and welfare.[9] The Reagan Administration's approach to federal health policy may be viewed as an example of a much larger strategy to realign federal and state relations, and dilute the relationship between government and the disadvantaged.

REFERENCES

1. §501 of the Social Security Act, 42 U.S.C. §705, et seq.

2. Earlier and less directed federal ventures into maternal and child health can be traced to Congressional establishment in 1912 of the Children's Bureau. The Bureau's extensive work on such issues as infant mortality, maternity care, and illegitimacy led to Congressional enactment of the Maternity and Infant Care Act of 1921 (the Sheppard-Towner Act), which provided federal maternal and child health grants to state health departments. The Act was repealed in 1929.

3. Medicaid and other federal health programs have been singularly responsible for closing the gap between rich and poor in access to necessary health care. Moreover, while it is difficult to demonstrate a direct causal link between the availability of medical care and improved health status, it is evident that the health of poor Americans began to improve dramatically after creation, beginning in the mid-1960s, of Medicaid and other health-related categorical programs such as the Women's Infant's and Children's Supplemental Feeding Program (WIC), expanded Title V services, and community and migrant health centers. For example, infant death rates among blacks dropped by 45% in 13 years; moreover there have been dramatic decreases in the rates of death from disease and conditions in which medical care is clearly beneficial, such as deaths during childbirth (72% decrease). See Rogers et al., "Who Needs Medicaid?" 307 *NEJMAG* 13 (July 1, 1982); Davis, Karen et al., *Health and the War on Poverty* (Brookings Institution, 1978); Health: United States (U.S. Department of Health and Human Services (PHS) 1979) pp. 112-132. *Budetti* et al., "Federal Health Program Reforms: Implications for Child Health, "60 *Millbank Memorial Fund Quarterly* 155, 165.

4. Unpublished 1980 data, United States Census Bureau.

5. Ibid.

6. Disadvantaged children have demonstrably greater health care needs, as evidenced by significantly higher infant mortality rates and lower health status measured by such indicators as loss of time in school, days of hospitalization and restricted activities due to chronic illness. *Budetti, op. cit* at p. 167.

7. Children's Defense Fund, *Portrait of Inequality: Black and White Children in America* (1980 pp. 88-106).

8. For example, during the 95th and 96th Congressional sessions based on information regarding the inadequacy of existing programs, the Carter Administration sought enactment of the Child Health Assurance Act (CHAP) which addressed some of the most serious gaps and deficiences in the Medicaid program for pregnant women and children. CHAP would have provided Medicaid coverage for a comprehensive range of services for poor children and pregnant women, regardless of their "categorical" eligibility (e.g., living in a home with only one parent) for federal financial assistance under the AFDC or SSI programs. For a variety of political reasons unrelated to the merits of the legislation, the bill failed to pass.

9. See, e.g., the Administration's Fiscal 1983 budget proposals which called for, *inter alia,* elimination of WIC and the summer food programs; a further tightening of AFDC eligibility provisions designed to assist the working poor, dramatic reductions in funding for elementary and secondary education; and other sweeping changes in federal social programs. Committee on the Budget, U.S. House of Representatives, *President Reagan's Fiscal 1983 Budget* (CP-12, U.S. Government Printing Office, Feb., 1982). For an example of the Administration's regulatory activities in health-related areas, see, 47 Fed. Reg. 33836 (proposed rules relaxing federal requirements for the Education for All Handicapped Children Programs).

Policy:
The Impact of Current Health Care Legislation on Poor Children and Families

Sara Rosenbaum, JD

ABSTRACT. This article reviews the Administration's national policy approach to maternal and child health. It offers an analysis of the Administration's legislative and regulatory efforts in this area, and concluded that the goal of the Administration has been to dilute and lessen the national maternal and child health commitment, at a time when recession, unemployment and new poverty have heightened the need for federal intervention. The purpose of this article is to describe the impact of the Reagan Administration's policy and administrative decisions on major federal health programs for poor children.

CHILDREN AND FEDERAL HEALTH PROGRAMS: ELIGIBILITY, UTILIZATION AND AVAILABILITY

Federal health programs are a web of legislation designed to plan, provide, and pay for the cost of delivering necessary health care for low-income, elderly or disabled Americans.[1] Domestic health programs accounted for over $75 billion in federal expenditures during Fiscal Year 1981, nearly 10% of the entire federal budget.[2] These programs address one of the most complex issues in domestic public policy—namely, the appropriate role of government in meeting the health needs of millions of persons excluded from the private health care system because of economic, racial, geographic or cultural barriers.[3]

Eligibility

While the maternal and child health portion of federal health expenditures is relatively modest,[4] the size of expenditures belies the heavy dependence by children and mothers on federal health programs, especially Medicaid. Low-income mothers and children are the very poorest of all Americans living in poverty. This phenomenon is chiefly the result of the failure of the major federal cash assistance program for poor children, Aid to Families with Dependent Children (AFDC), to keep pace with inflation. The federalized cash assistance programs for the elderly and the handicapped (including Social Security and Supplemental Security Income), by contrast, have been indexed to inflation.[5] In certain states, the disparity in income levels between children and the elderly is substantial; for example, a single elderly person living in Texas can have a monthly income of approximately $300 and qualify for Medicaid. A child in Texas, living in a 4-member family, can qualify for AFDC, and therefore Medicaid, only if his (and each other family member's) income does not exceed $35.00 per month.

Such extraordinarily low eligibility levels, as well as restrictive categorical requirements under the AFDC and Medicaid programs, mean that in many states, a large percentage of families living below federal poverty levels receive no Medicaid and cannot afford to purchase any health care. Moreover, unlike the elderly and disabled indigent children families are ineligible for Medicare; and a substantial percentage of children under 18 possess no health insurance at all.[6] They rely heavily on free public health programs. Furthermore, the number of uninsured children relying on free public health care will grow as unemployment increases and as Medicaid reaches fewer children as a result of cutbacks in federal welfare programs.

Despite their limited eligibility, those low-income children who do qualify for health insurance under Medicaid depend disproportionately on the aid it provides. Whereas Medicaid represented 25 cents out of every public dollar spent on the elderly in 1979, it represented some 55 cents of every public dollar spent on children.[7]

Utilization and Availability

Poor children's extreme poverty and uninsuredness is evident in their significant underutilization of health services, especially preventive and primary services. The rate of underutilization increases significantly when utilization rates are adjusted for disadvantaged children's poorer health status.[8] While a lack of insurance probably accounts for some of this underutilization, the unavailability of appropriate health services for the poor, especially those living in inner city or rural areas, is also a major contributing factor.[9] Not surprisingly, the majority of services rendered by local health departments to more than 72 million persons during Fiscal Year 1979 were maternal and child health-related services,[10] while approximately half of all persons served by the federal Community and Migrant Health Centers programs are children.[11] In many states, however, health departments provide far less than comprehensive care, while community health centers reach only 6 million of the more than 20 million Americans living in medically underserved areas.[12]

Thus, all evidence shows that in 1980, health programs for poor children were reaching too few, and were providing inadequate levels of services given their greater health care needs. These facts only intensified when recession and unemployment combined to swell the ranks of low-income children. Yet, health programs affecting children were an early target of the Reagan Administration. The cost of federal health programs alone does not explain the Administration's position. Indeed, many of the Administration's most important efforts to reduce federal health programs for children were aimed at cost-effective preventive services, such as immunizations. Thus, the Administration's proposals have had only secondary budget implications. They instead reflect a fundamental philosophical opposition to the concept of governmental obligation to strive for basic equity in access to health care by all poor children. Furthermore, the Administration has offered no alternative approach to meeting maternal and child health needs to take the place of the existing public system.

THE REAGAN ADMINISTRATION'S LEGISLATIVE STRATEGY

Budgetary Changes

The Reagan Administration's legislative agenda in health has been sweeping. Virtually no federal health program affecting children has remained untouched. Each program has been attacked by both the annual federal budget process or through the more long range "New Federalism" initiative. (See Table 1)

During the federal budget debates for fiscal years 1982 and 1983, the Administration was relatively unsuccessful in its efforts to achieve substantial redirections in the content and philosophy of the largest federal health programs. The Administration was quite successful, however, in persuading Congress to make substantial spending reductions at a time when the growing recession was already forcing states to dramatically scale back their own social welfare budgets.[13] Because poor children depend so heavily on federally funded programs and tend to fare poorly in many states when

TABLE 1: The Reagr , Administration's Legislative Strategy

```
┌─────────────────────┐  ┌──────────────────────────┐  ┌──────────────────────────┐
│ BUDGETARY CHANGES:  │  │ LEGISLATIVE CHANGES:     │  │ REGULATORY REFORMS:      │
│                     │  │                          │  │                          │
│ All federal child   │  │ The Omnibus Budget       │  │ Retained safeguards &    │
│  health programs    │  │  Reconciliation Act      │  │  standards               │
│  had budgetary      │  │  (OBRA/1981)             │  │ Relaxed federal          │
│  reductions         │  │ Tax Equity & Fiscal      │  │  regulatory standards    │
│                     │  │  Responsibility Act      │  │ Eliminated procedural    │
│                     │  │  (TEFRA/1982)            │  │  protections             │
└─────────────────────┘  └──────────────────────────┘  └──────────────────────────┘
                                       │
                         ┌──────────────────────────┐
                         │ PROVIDED REDUCTIONS IN:  │
                         │                          │
                         │ Title V Maternal & Child │
                         │ Health Block Grants,     │
                         │ Community & Migrant Health│
                         │ Centers, Federal         │
                         │ Immunization Programs.   │
                         └──────────────────────────┘
                                       │
                         ┌──────────────────────────┐
                         │ PROVIDED A BASE FOR:     │
                         │                          │
                         │ Overall reduction of     │
                         │ medicaid.                │
                         └──────────────────────────┘
                                       │
                         ┌──────────────────────────┐
                         │ PROVIDED STRUCTURAL      │
                         │ IMPROVEMENTS FOR:        │
                         │                          │
                         │ Medicaid incentives for  │
                         │  home-based care         │
                         │ Improved medical &       │
                         │  health related services │
                         │ Complete protection for  │
                         │  pregnant women &        │
                         │  children                │
                         │ Liberalized eligibility  │
                         │  standards               │
                         └──────────────────────────┘
```

non-federal budget allocation decisions are made,[14] the potential impact of this redirection in federal spending patterns is enormous.[14a]

Legislative Changes

Key legislative changes in federal health programs affecting mothers and children are reflected in a two-fold trend: The Omnibus Budget Reconciliation Act (OBRA) of 1981,[15] and the Tax Equity Act of 1982 (TEFRA)[16] provide for overall spending reductions in the federal Medicaid budget of more than $4 billion between fiscal years 1982 and 1985. Most of these budget reductions have been achieved, however, by restructuring the federal matching formula under Medicaid and through other means that only indirectly affect beneficiaries.[17] This is a decisively different approach from that taken by the Administration, which sought to completely restructure the Medicaid program by placing a flat cap on federal expenditures and stripping away beneficiary protections.[18]

With respect to other health programs for children, the Omnibus Budget Reconciliation Act of 1981 resulted in spending reductions of from 12%-20% in programs such as the Title V Maternal and Child Health Block Grant, Community and Migrant Health Centers, and federal immunization programs.[19] These budget reductions were accompanied by legislation designed to replace certain existing categorical programs, such as the Title V maternal and Child Health and Crippled Children's and Community Health Centers programs with block grant programs.[20] In no case, however, was the resulting legislation as dramatic a revision in federal health policy as were the Administration's original legislative proposals. Indeed, the restructured Title V Block Grant, while removing certain key safeguards,[20a] also improved the previous program in several respects.[21] Furthermore, Congress never even seriously considered the Administration's proposals for Fiscal 1983, which would have involved placing the Title V and WIC programs in the same block grant and cutting their funding levels by 25%.

Structural Changes

Finally, Congress made limited but important improvements in the Medicaid program under OBRA and TEFRA. These include: new incentives to states to provide home-based, enriched medical and health-related services to Medicaid beneficiaries who would otherwise need institutionalization;[22] complete protection for all pregnant women and children receiving Medicaid from copayment requirements for pregnancy-related and pediatric care;[23] and liberalized eligibility standards under Medicaid which states can utilize at their option in order to provide home-based care to handicapped children otherwise at risk of institutionalization.[24]

Proposed New Federalism

Beyond its Fiscal 1982 and 1983 budget proposals, the Administration's major domestic policy initiative has been its New Federalism program. While details of the proposal have changed over time, the Administration has generally proposed to assume responsibility for much of Medicaid, in exchange for states' assumption of the entire cost of the AFDC program.[25] Additionally, New Federalism calls for a "turnback" of numerous discretionary health and human service programs, to be funded until 1990 by a Federal Trust Fund.[26] The Trust Fund would then disappear, leaving states responsible for generating their own revenues for the "turnback" programs.[27]

While the terms of New Federalism are currently being debated at the national level, preliminary indications are that the Administration's proposals are unacceptable to the states, in great part because of its unwillingness to agree to establish and finance a federal Medicaid program that would ensure adequate levels of health insurance for low-income Americans.[28] As with the Administration's other health policy proposals and actions, its New Federalism Medicaid initiative reflects a philosophy of diluting the federal government's obligation to ensure access by the poor to basic health and human services.

Congress' Resistance to Legislative Changes

Thus, while funding for federal health programs has been seriously reduced, actual structural changes have been relatively moderate; indeed, in some cases existing statutory protections have actually been improved. However, two factors probably account for Congress' ultimate refusal to make the broad policy changes sought by the White House.

First, because of the high cost and high-stakes politics of federal health legislation, Congress has generally moved in a cautious and incremental fashion. Programs such as Medicare and Medicaid, for example, have been heavily influenced and shaped by the concerns of the American health care industry, and have taken decades to evolve into their current pattern of complex and delicately balanced interests. This political protection for the programs is enhanced by the slow and deliberate nature of the Congressional process, with numerous steps between the introduction of legislation and final passage.

While the 1974 passage of the federal Budget Act through its "reconciliation"[29] provisions, provides a means for speeding up the legislative process in times of perceived economic crisis, as in 1981 and 1982, the health program changes that were ultimately enacted did demonstrate Congress' concerns about making precipitous and fundamental changes in health legislation, especially where no alternatives were offered to take the place of existing programs. This hesitancy was probably reinforced by the fact that the creation of some of the Administration's proposed block grants would have potentially realigned Committee jurisdiction over sensitive programs.[30]

Second, because of the magnitude of federal spending involved, both the health care industry, and state, and local officials opposed many of the Administration's health proposals, especially that of putting a flat limit on the availability of federal Medicaid funds. As a result of enormous pressure by governors, local officials, state legislators, the health care industry, and consumer advocates during the so-called "Gramm-Latta" budget reconciliation debate of 1981,[31] the Republicans were forced to withdraw from consideration their health "reform" package, which included not only the Medicaid "cap" proposal, but all of the Administration's health block grant and other health proposals, as well.[32]

In sum, despite the fact that the Administration has been relatively unsuccessful in its effort to achieve a fundamental redirection in federal health legislative policy, it has succeeded in generating numerous damaging changes. More importantly, it has been able to win major spending reductions at the very time that states—and the poor—are least able to absorb federal budget cuts.

THE REAGAN ADMINISTRATION'S REGULATORY REFORMS

While the Administration's public health policies have achieved less legislative success than anticipated, its "regulatory reform" efforts have been successful, comprehensive, and will substantially affect the content, quality, and operation of the nation's most important federal health programs. If the Administration's failure to legislatively alter federal health programs continues, the area of regulatory action may become the increasing focus of its attempts to reshape federal health policy for the poor.

One of the Reagan Administration's chief concerns has been over the "intrusiveness" of federal regulations into state and local and private sector decision-making processes, even where such regulations are necessary to fulfill statutory entitlements and advance vital health and safety concerns. As part of the Administration's push for "regulatory reform," the President, soon after assuming office, established a government-wide Regulatory Reform Task Force[33] to uncover "administrative waste and burdensomeness" in federal regulations. Health regulations were prominent on the Task Force's agenda, since federal health rules contain numerous and prescriptive requirements governing everything from complex eligibility determination regulations under Medicaid to comprehensive standards for nursing homes. Health regulations were, in short, an embodiment of all that the Administration found wrong with federal agency conduct.

Beyond their inconsistency with the Administration's philosophy, health regulations attracted the Administration's attention for "practical" reasons. In many instances, the new federal health regulations substantially "flesh out" ambiguous statutory schemes, frequently using a mandate from Congress to set standards or an otherwise undefined word or phrase.[34] For example, Medicaid statutory provisions are frequently obscure, complicated, or ambiguous. The federal regulations, however, provide hundreds of pages of detailed, formal directions to states regarding how eligibility is to be determined, what services must be provided and how the program is to be administered. Generally, regulations give scope and content to unclear statutory directives by defining minimum services, eligibility, state administrative procedures, or standards for facilities. Thus, while the Administration may not have been able to achieve broad philosophical redirections in health by legislative means, it encountered fertile, and seemingly vulnerable, ground among health regulations, many of which are discretionary and susceptible to dilution.

The Administration's regulatory efforts affecting health programs for mothers and children can be classified under three major categories: (a) where Congress has, in the face of strong Administration opposition, either retained *statutory safeguards* and *standards* or has added additional ones, the Administration has sought to implement the resulting legislation *as if* its initial legislative aims had been achieved, thereby severely undercutting the integrity of both the protections and the legislative process, (b) the Administration has repeatedly attempted to use its regulatory authority to *relax* and *eliminate existing federal regulatory standards,* even in situations in which Congress has reaffirmed its approval of those standards, and (c) and in order to ensure swift achievement of its "regulatory reform" goals, the Administration has sought to *eliminate exceedingly important procedural protections for* both *program beneficiaries* and the general public, which have been adhered to by both Democratic and Republican Administrations alike. Below is a comprehensive discussion on these three major categories.

Standards and Protections

During both the Fiscal 1982 and 1983 budget debates, Congress maintained important substantive and procedural safeguards in federal health programs and added additional new protections for children. For example, in 1981, Congress rejected the Administration's "no-strings" legislative proposals for maternal and child health, and instead enacted the Title V Maternal and Child Health Block Grant, which includes a series of important safeguards and guarantees.[35] Despite this strong show of Congressional concern for protecting health services for mothers and children and ensuring program accountability, however, federal regulations implementing the Title V Block Grant[36] reflect none of this. With the exception of general federal regulations applicable to all of the 1981 block grant programs, there is not a single regulation governing the Title V program, even though the law contains numerous eligibility, service, procedural, reporting, and civil rights requirements sufficiently complex to require further interpretation and refinement.[38]

The Department's final block grant rules leave no doubt that its philosophy is to treat the Title V Block Grant (as well as the other newly-enacted block grant programs) as if the Administration's original block grant proposals (which, not coincidentally, did not include a separate maternal and child health block grant) had been enacted. This has been true even where, as under Title V, specific provisions of the new law necessitate the establishment of federal standards:

> The Secretary has determined that the Department should implement the block grant programs in a manner that is fully consistent with the Congressional intent to enlarge the States' ability to control use of the funds involved. Accordingly, to the extent possible, we will not burden the States' administration of the programs with definitions of permissible and prohibited activities, procedural rules, paperwork and recordkeeping requirements, or other regulatory provisions. The States will, for the most part, be subject only to the statutory requirements, and the Department will carry out its functions with due regard for the limited nature of the role that Congress has assigned to us.[39]

It is not only Title V beneficiaries who stand to be harmed by this failure to provide regulatory guidance. State health departments risk loss of federal funding if their programs are found to be out of compliance with federal requirements, and therefore need further guidance. Furthermore, as legislatures and Executives in fiscally hard-hit states search for areas in which they can achieve needed spending reductions, it is far easier to find additional savings from programs whose requirements are so vague, and whose enforcement is so lax, that any minimal effort will suffice.

With respect to Medicaid, a similar pattern of Administration disregard for the terms of newly-enacted legislation has emerged. For example, as part of its fiscal year 1982 Medicaid legislative package, the Administration sought a complete relaxation of Federal statutory provisions specifying procedures states must follow in determining the financial eligibility of "medically needy" Medicaid applicants.[40] Congress specifically rejected this proposal and retained existing financial eligibility standards.[41] Yet, purportedly for the purpose of implementing the fiscal 1982 Medicaid legislative changes, the Department issued final rules that virtually eliminated the financial eligibility protections that Congress had preserved, and promulgated standards that parallelled its original legislative proposals which Congress had rejected.[42]

Substantial Relaxation of Existing Regulatory Protections

The Administration has pressed repeatedly to downgrade or repeal important regulatory protections under a wide array of health programs. Frequently, these regulatory efforts have parallelled the

Administration's efforts to repeal the programs legislatively. For example, in 1981, the Administration proposed to repeal major portions of the Medicaid Early and Periodic Screening Diagnosis and Treatment (EPSDT) statute, the nation's largest preventive health program for poor children.[43] This proposal was rejected. Preliminary proposals to repeal the program entirely were put forth in 1982 as well, once again with no success.[44] In early 1982, however, the Department drafted new EPSDT regulations which would have virtually eliminated many of the program's most important regulatory requirements, including the provision of detailed assessments, immunizations, scheduling, transportation, and effective outreach services.[45] The Department's deregulation efforts were halted after a major public outcry ensued; instead, the agency has resorted to a more invisible strategy of simply refusing to enforce current regulations, and of illegal and informal communications to states instructing them that existing rules are no longer in force.[45a]

Similar Administration strategies of simultaneously pressing for the repeal of legislation while at the same time moving to deregulate existing requirements, have surfaced under the Hill Burton,[46] Community Health Centers,[47] and Family Planning[48] programs. Often, as in the case of the Department's EPSDT proposals, the attempt to deregulate has been overt; at other times, as in the case of Community Health Centers, the approach has been more subtle.[49] In all cases it has become clear to outside observers that the Administration intends to do by regulation that which Congress has precluded legislatively.

Efforts to Terminate Procedural Protections for Program Beneficiaries and the Public

Even more disturbing, perhaps, than the Administration's attempts to modify substantive regulations, have been its efforts to repeal procedural protections that ensure the integrity of the federal rulemaking process itself, as well as the constitutionality and fairness of governmental actions affecting public program beneficiaries. Indeed, the protections attacked by the Administration are not only the products of decades of legislative and administrative policy, but arise under the United States Constitution itself.

With respect to rules affecting the regulatory process, in May 1982, the Administration issued regulations significantly limiting access to public documents guaranteed under the Freedom of Information Act.[50] Such access has been a critical tool in effective advocacy. Moreover, in June 1982, the Administration proposed to invoke a little-known exemption under the Administrative Procedure Act that would permit the agency to issue final regulations affecting all public benefit programs (including Medicare, Medicaid, Social Security, AFDC, and Supplemental Security Income, to name only a few) without first affording the public advance notice and the opportunity to comment on its proposals.[51] The proposals furthermore sought to prohibit judicial review of any Department decision to bypass notice and comment, and relaxed the standards the agency would have to meet in determining whether it was appropriate to forego a comment period.[52]

With respect to regulations ensuring the fairness of federal and state administrative decisions to deny or reduce benefits to beneficiaries of public programs, including the more than 10 million children receiving AFDC and/or Medicaid, the Administration has sought to relax federal safeguards to the point that constitutional or policy questions of the most fundamental nature are raised. In March 1982, for example, the Department issued two sets of related rules[53] that proposed to repeal all regulatory protections governing federally-funded experiments on millions of recipients of public benefits including Medicaid, AFDC, Supplemental Security Income, Head Start, Title V Maternal and Child Health Block Grant services and many more. Under the Department's proposals, federal or state officials could, under the guise of "experimentation," conduct large-scale social "experiments" to deny crucial medical and health-related benefits otherwise guaranteed by federal law, without first having to ensure that the experiments were safe, just and ethical. The regulatory standards at issue grew out of the Nuremburg War Crimes Trials,[54] and have been viewed by courts and Congress alike as applying with special force to Medicaid and other public program beneficiaries—the very poor and minority individuals most likely to be victimized by unethical and unsafe experimentation.[55]

In addition to this large-scale proposal, the Department has permitted states to conduct experiments involving the denial of Medicaid and other health-related benefits to thousands of persons (including pregnant women and children) by summarily withholding benefits without advance notice to beneficiaries of the reductions, and without providing recipients an opportunity to oppose the denial of assistance.[56] Timely notice and the opportunity for a prereduction hearing under federal welfare programs have been viewed by the United States Supreme Court as basic tenets of the United States Constitution for over a decade.[57]

In conclusion, the Reagan Administration's legislative regulatory approach to federal child health programs has shown itself to far surpass any legitimate need for budgetary constraints. The Administration's legislative and administrative recommendations, proposals and actions demonstrate distinct ideological opposition toward national standards, protections, and perhaps most importantly, enforceable rights. The Administration's ultimate success remains to be seen, but the impact of its actions on the lives of a generation of disadvantaged children are already being felt nationwide.

REFERENCES

1. Some of the most important programs affecting mothers and children include Medicaid (Title XIX of the Social Security Act, 42 U.S.C. §1396, *et seq.*); the Title V Maternal and Child Health Block Grant program (Title V of the Social Security Act, 42 U.S.C. §701, *et seq.* The law was amended in 1981 by Title XXI of P.L. 97-35 to include the Title V maternal and child health and crippled children's programs, the SSI/Disabled Children's Program, special categorical programs for treatment of hemophilia, sudden infant death syndrome and genetic disorders, adolescent pregnancy programs, and lead-based paint poisoning); the Hill-Burton program (Title XVI of the Public Health Service Act, 42 U.S.C. §300 p); the Community Health Centers program (Title 330 of the Public Health Service, 42 U.S.C. §254c, as amended in 1981 by title IX of Pub. L. 97-35); and the Migrant Health Centers program, §329 of the Public Health Service Act, 42 U.S.C. §254d.

2. *Health Care Financing Review* (Sept. 1982) (HCFA/DHHS, Baltimore, MD).

3. For an excellent discussion of the politics of the American public health care system, see, Stevens and Stevens, *Welfare Medicine in America* (Free Press, 1974).

4. For example, children comprise nearly half of all Medicaid recipients, but payments on their behalf are only about 19% of Medicaid expenditures. Expenditures for children drop as low as 11.3% of all payments in New Hampshire. Office of Research and Demonstrations, *The Medicare and Medicaid Data Book: 1981* (HCFA/DHHS, 1981) at pp. 76, 107. Moreover, when rates of expenditure increase are adjusted for inflation, there has actually been a net loss in federal health expenditures for children. *Budetti, op. cit.* at p. 158.

5. *Budetti, op. cit.,* at p. 164.

6. Medicaid reaches only about half of all families living in poverty because of restrictive eligibility requirements. HCFA, *Data on the Medicaid Program,* FY 1979 (ORD/HCFA/HHS, Baltimore, MD), p. 61. It is estimated that approximately 12% of all children under 18 have no health insurance, public or private. Furthermore, they are disproportionately uninsured. Children under 18 comprise 32.8% of the United States population, but comprise 38.4% of the uninsured population. Congress of the United States, *Profile of Health Care Coverage: The Haves and Have-Nots* (CSRO, March 1979).

7. *Budetti, op. cit.,* at p.

8. *Kleinman* et al., "Use of Ambulatory Medical Care by the Poor: Another Look At Equity, "XIX *Medical Care* 1011, 1016-1019. Furthermore, underutilization is especially evident for minorities.

9. Davis, Karen "Primary Care for the Medically Underserved: Public and Private Financing," (Johns Hopkins, Baltimore, 1981).

10. ASTHO, *Comprehensive NPHPRS Report: Services, Expenditures and Programs of State and Territorial Health Agencies,* FY 1979 (ASTHO Pub. No. 56, ND) at p. 51.

11. Unpublished data, National Association of Community Health Centers, Washington, D.C.

12. Davis, Karen, *op. cit.*

13. In 1981, even before the first round of federal budget cuts began, 31 states had already considered reducing or had actually reduced the scope of their Medicaid programs. *A Children's Defense Budget* (CDF), 1982, p. 52).

14. A review of social welfare expenditures in Texas, for example, reveals that, except for state expenditures mandated by federal program requirements, disproportionately few funds were spent on non-education programs for poor children. The rate of expenditures was projected to fall even lower in the absence of federal spending requirements, Grubb, W. Norton et al., Public Expenditures for Children and Youth," *Public Affairs Comment* (University of Texas at Austin, Vol XXVIII, No. 3).

14a. Fifty-five American cities have recently reported that, as a result of federal budget cuts, they are less able to cope with their population's health needs than with any other human service. At the very time that they are being asked to provide greater levels of free health for the poor, these cities are reporting a 10% drop in the number of persons they can afford to serve.

15. Pub. L. 97-35.

16. Pub. L. 97-248.

17. For example, OBRA gave states broad new flexibility to establish progressive rate-setting systems for both hospitals and nursing homes. Section 2173, Pub. L. 97-35.

While it is true that many of the OBRA and TEFRA changes did not directly affect beneficiaries, this is not to suggest that Medicaid recipients are not harmed by provider controls and arrangements that result in too little or poor quality care. For an excellent discussion of the impact of poorly controlled provider reimbursement arrangements on Medicaid beneficiaries see Chavkin, David, "California's Prepaid Health Program: Can the Patient Be Saved?" 28 Hastings Law Journal 685 (Jan., 1977).

Furthermore, both TEFRA and OBRA made numerous and damaging changes in existing protections for millions of Medicaid beneficiaries. Under certain OBRA amendments, states may now deny Medicaid eligibility to certain categories of beneficiaries and cut back on the amount of services they were previously required to provide. Sec. 2171, Pub. L. 97-35. TEFRA changes include new authority for states to impose liens on the homes of chronically ill beneficiaries in order to recover the cost of care and the right to impose onerous cost-sharing requirements on millions of Medicaid recipients previously protected from copayments. Sections 131 and 132, Publ. L. 97-248.

18. The Administration's proposed, H.R. 3725 (introduced on May 28, 1981), would have diluted the entitlement characteristics of the Medicaid statute and replaced them with an annual maximum appropriation, to be increased at a certain rate each year. While the House of Representatives rejected this approach and instead chose to alter the federal formula for reimbursing states (H.R. 3982), the Senate did vote to impose a somewhat more generous ceiling than that proposed by the President.

A Medicaid "cap," had it succeeded, would have profoundly altered the philosophical, legal, budgetary and practical aspects of the program. Such a plan would have brought into serious question beneficiaries' claims of entitlement to benefits, and subjected the major health care financing program for the poor to an arbitrary limitation on growth not necessarily linked in a reasonable fashion to the rate of growth in the cost of medical care. It would have thereby subjected both states and major Medicaid providers to a potential crisis in which available funds to care for the poor would have been even more grossly inadequate. Many states would have understandably responded with even greater efforts to limit Medicaid expenditures for the poor. Given children's disproportionate reliance on the program and their tendency to rely heavily on the very services that carry the least political weight (e.g., clinical care and general outpatient services), the youngest part of the Medicaid population would have probably suffered the most heavily. See Budetti, *op. cit.*

19. The Fiscal Year 1982 funding reductions were: Community Health Centers: 23.3% below FY 1981 levels, Migrant Health Centers: 11.8% below FY 1981 funding levels, Title V Block grant (including title V and related programs): 23.8% below FY 1981 funding levels, Immunizations: 6.9% below FY 1981 funding levels.

20. Titles IX and XXI of Pub. L. 97-35.

20a. The most important requirement eliminated by Congress in 1981 was a provision mandating all states to maintain "programs of projects," which were special comprehensive health clinics for pregnant women, infants, children and youth. 42 U.S.C. sec. 705 (1980). During 1982, 35-40 states took advantage of this new flexibility to reduce or eliminate their programs of projects. Hundreds of thousands of mothers and children have been affected.

21. For example, the Administration's original Fiscal Year Budget requests included no separate Maternal and Child Health Block Grant. Funds for serving mothers and children would have been included in a very broad "primary care" block grant. Similarly, the Administration's proposals would have eliminated from all of the proposed block grants state matching and earmarking requirements (such as the requirements found in the Title V block grant that states spend certain proportions of funds for certain services and provide a level of matching funds) as well as any beneficiary protections (such as prohibitions against costsharing by low-income persons ultimately included by Congress in the Title V block grant). See, 127 Cong. Rec. (House) June 26, 1981 (pp. H3927, et seq.)

22. §2175, Pub. L. 97-35.

23. §131, Pub. L. 97-248.

24. §134, Pub. L. 97-248.

25. Administration budget papers, Fiscal 1983. See also, CDF, *A Children's Defense Budget*, op. cit., at p. 48.

26. Ibid.

27. Ibid.

28. For example, Administration proposals in June 1982, failed to include any medically needy program and contained inadequate funding for longterm care.

29. §310, Pub. L. 93-344, Congressional Budget and Impoundment Act of 1974.

30. For example, as part of its Fiscal 1983 budget request, the Administration called for the block-granting of the Title V and WIC programs. A not inconsiderable barrier to this proposal (which soon died for various reasons) was that it could potentially have meant the loss of jurisdiction over WIC by the Senate and House Agriculture Committees, both of which have been supportive of the program's goals and funding and justifiably proud of its achievements.

31. See note 26, *supra,* for citation of Gramm-Latta debate.

32. 127 Cong. Rec. 2983 (statement by Mr. Broyhill, withdrawing his amendment). As with all political events, however, the story is not so simply told. In fact, the Democratic health package may have succeeded in great measure because the House Energy and Commerce Committee (which has jurisdiction over Medicaid, portions of Medicare, and nearly all discretionary and civilian health programs) was unable to report a bill for inclusion in the House Budget Committee's omnibus package, which ultimately lost to the Republican substitute. Had there not been a separate debate on the health package, which itself was a larger part of energy and commerce package, it might have been far more difficult for the large health interests to persuade sufficient Congressmen to vote to amend or defeat the Republican substitute. (Sugar subsidies too).

33. Executive Order 12291.

34. For example, the Medicaid early and periodic screening diagnosis and treatment (EPSDT) statute specifically empowers the Secretary with administrative authority to establish rules defining the medical content and scope of the program, 42 U.S.C. §1396d(a) (4) (B).

35. See note 30, *supra.*

36. Interim final rules were issued on October 1, 1981 (46 Fed. Reg. 48582). Final rules were issued on July 6, 1982 (47 Fed. Reg. 29472).

37. 45 CFR §§96.10-96.68.

38. For example, the Title V Block Grant requires that states spend a "substantial" portion of funds on health services and a "reasonable" proportion in primary care. 42 U.S.C. §705. Although there is some legislative history with respect to the meaning of more terms, the statute itself provides no guidance as to how the terms should be interpreted. The Secretary chose to leave the terms undefined. Additionally, the new block grant, 42 U.S.C. §704, prohibits states from using Title V funds to provide important care outside of limited circumstances. Although asked to do so, the Secretary refused to define permissible uses of inpatient hospital services. See, generally, 47 Fed. Reg. 29484.

Moreover, the 1981 statutory amendments added nondiscrimination provisions that for the first time prohibit discrimination on the basis of sex or religion, 42 U.S.C. §708. No federal regulations have yet been issued to implement these provisions, even though it has been evident from years of civil rights enforcement activities under Title VI of the 1965 Civil Rights Act and §504 of the Developmental Disabilities and Bill of Rights Act of 1973, that in the area of health care, discrimination by state agencies, providers, and other entities involved in the health delivery system for the poor is often subtle and pervasive. See, generally, Institute of Medicine, Health Care in a Context of Civil Rights (Academy of Sciences, National Academy Press, Washington, D.C.).

39. 46 Fed. Reg. 48583.

40. §102 (c), H.R. 3725 (introduced May 28, 1981).

41. Indeed, Congressional concern that the Administration adhere to these protections was so substantial that two of the principal Medicaid conferees, Congressman Henry Waxman and Senator Robert Dole, offered floor statements amending the House/Senate Medicaid Conference report contained in Pub. L. 97-35 to further clarify their intentions. 127 Cong. Rec. 59218.

42. The Tax Equity and Fiscal Responsibility Act of 1983 specifically repudiates these regulations and clarifies Congressional intent that the financial eligibility standards for the medically needy are to remain untouched. See, H.R. Rep. 97-757 (to accompany H.R. 6877), pp. 13-14.

43. Administration bill cited at note 37.

44. Fiscal 1983 Administration budget papers.

45. Unpublished draft, 3/82.

45a. State Medicaid Manual HCFA Pub. 45-5 §5010.

46. The Hill Burton program, Title XVI of the Public Health Services Act, was enacted in 1947 and has provided billions of dollars in federal loans and grants for hospital construction and renovation. In exchange for federal funds, hospitals receiving aid have guaranteed that they will provide a reasonable volume of free care to persons unable to pay and will serve the community in which they operate. For over a decade, low-income and civil rights advocates have sought to enforce these guarantees. In 1979, the federal government issued comprehensive regulations detailing hospitals' free care and community service obligations. 44 Fed. Reg. (May 18, 1979). These regulations were bitterly opposed by hospitals, which unsuccessfully sought to have the rules overturned. *AHA v. Schweiker.*

In 1981, the Administration's legislative package (bill cited at note 37) included an outright repeal of the Hill Burton Act. That effort failed. In 1982, it was revealed that the Administration was drafting new Hill Burton rules which would substantially dilute many of the most important regulatory guarantees. Unpublished draft.

47. During 1981 the Reagan Administration unsuccessfully sought to repeal the Community Health Centers Program, Section 330 of the Public Health Service Act, one of the most important pieces of federal legislation for creating comprehensive health services for medically underserved populations. Although Congress did replace the program with the Primary Care Block Grant Act, Title IX of Pub. L. 97-35, many conditions and protections were included in the Act in order to ensure the survival and integrity of CHCS.

The Administration immediately sought to achieve its original goals through both regulatory action and inaction. First, it refused to promulgate any regulations implementing the new Act, leaving states with no guidance as to the meaning of the law's requirements and guarantees. 47 Fed. Reg. 29472 (July 6, 1982). This refusal to issue rules was specifically rejected by Congress which, in acting on the Orphan Drug Act (H.R. 5328) in October, 1982, amended the law to require the Administration to promulgate specific Primary Care Block Grant rules.

The Administration has also taken affirmative regulatory action to undercut existing CHCS. Centers can be developed only in areas that are officially designated as medically underserved, 42 U.S.C. 254c. In early 1982, the Administration issued restrictive new standards for determining when an area is underserved that are resulting in the decertification (and defunding) of numerous Community Health Centers. 47 Fed. Reg. 25828 (1982).

48. The Reagan Administration has repeatedly sought to abolish the Family Planning Act, Title X of the Public Health Service Act. See, e.g., Administration bill cited at note 37. Having failed to secure a repeal of the law, the Administration proposed in early 1982 stringent new federal regulations requiring parental notification before minors could receive ongoing family planning services. 47 Fed. Reg. 7699 (1982). Experts in the field believe that these rules, if finalized, will virtually prevent family planning clinics from effectively treating adolescents. Adolescent pregnancy is one of the leading causes of infant mortality and morbidity, because of the young mother's extremely high-risk status.

49. See note 56.

50. 47 Fed. Reg. 20309 (May 12, 1982). The change was summarily implemented without opportunity for comment.

51. 5 U.S.C. §553(a) (2) ordinarily exempts from APA rulemaking procedural requirements (such as publication of proposed rules with a comment period, delayed effectiveness of final rules, and the right to petition for regulatory change) rules pertaining to public benefits, grants, contracts, and loans. This exemption, known as the "proprietary exemption" has been viewed for at least 15 years as an obsolete exemption which harkens back to the time when government benefits were viewed as largesse rather than a right and, therefore, not deserving of any procedural due process protections. Numerous pieces of Congressional legislation have sought to eliminate this exemption. See, generally, Bonfeld, "Public Participation in Federal Rulemaking Relating to Public Property, Loans, Grants, Benefits or Contracts" 118 U. Penn. Law Review 540 (1970).

This particular proposal by the Administration raises special concerns, since it suggests that the Administration in fact views its responsibilities under public benefit programs as mere largesse to be dispensed or removed at will. Such a position has been thoroughly discredited by both Congress and Courts for over a decade.

52. Since the United States Constitution's due process requirements govern federal agency action, and since Congress, not federal agencies, determines the jurisdiction of the federal courts, this aspect of the Department's notice is perhaps the most difficult to understand.

53. 47 Fed. Reg. 9208 (March 4, 1982); 47 Fed. Reg. 12276 March 22, 1982).

54. National Commission for the Protection of Human Subjects of Biomedical and Behavioral Research, *The Belmont Reports*, (Washington, D.C. 1978).

55. See, e.g., *Crane v. Matthews*, 417 F. Supp. 432 (N.D. Ga. 1976). As part of the 1982 Tax Equity and Fiscal Responsibility Act of 1982 (section 131(b)), Pub. L. 97-128), Congress, in response to the Administration's abuse of its experimental authority severely restricted its ability to conduct such experiments.

56. See letter from Dr. Carolyne Davis to Jeffrey Miller, Director, Illinois Department of Public Aid (March 11, 1982) which permitted the state, under its §1115 Medicaid "experiment" to reduce beneficiaries' Medicaid coverage without timely and adequate notice and without an opportunity for a prereduction hearing.

57. *Goldberg v. Kelly,* 397 U.S. 254 (1970).

Practice:
Maternal and Child Health in America:
Toward a Model Local Program

Robert L. Goldenberg, MD
Kathleen G. Nelson, MD

ABSTRACT. The many federal programs targeted at improving the health of children and pregnant women, Medicaid is identified as the major funding program. Others, such as the Maternal and Child Health, and Community Health Center Programs were created to increase the state's or community's capacity to provide health services. The major problems of fragmentation of services and the absence of capacity to provide care due to a lack of poor distribution of resources are discussed. A model program is described which would pool available resources and designate a single "health care home" for children and pregnant women. In addition, linkages with appropriate referral and tertiary care agencies would be developed to care for medical problems beyond the capabilities of the local agency.

INTRODUCTION

The development of a model program to improve child health must be based on an understanding of the history of federal child health programs and on the structure of the existing local health care delivery system upon which the federal health programs will be superimposed. This paper, therefore, will describe some of the most important federal legislation impacting on child health, and examine

---

From the departments of Obstetrics and Gynecology and Pediatrics at the University of Alabama in Birmingham.

Reprint request to: Robert L. Goldenberg, Department of Obstetrics and Gynecology, the University of Alabama in Birmingham, University Station, Birmingham, Alabama 35294.

some of the most obvious difficulties in translating the federal legislation into effective health care for the nation's children. Working
within the existing federal legislative framework, the components of
a model health care system aimed at improving the health of the nation's children will be described.

This paper deals not only with child health but health care to pregnant women as well, because the provision of health services to the
mother and unborn child is intimately related to child health status.
For example, 80% of the mortality in the first year of life is related
to events preceding delivery.[1] In addition nearly all of the federal
child health programs address maternal health as well as child
health.

FEDERAL INVOLVEMENT IN MATERNAL
AND CHILD HEALTH

The federal government's involvement in child health began in
1912 with the development of the Children's Bureau and continued
in 1935 with the passage of Title V of the Social Security Act (see
Table 1, page 4). This section of the federal social security legislation made funds available to the states "for the purpose of enabling
each state to extend and improve, especially in rural areas and in
areas suffering from severe economic distress: 1) services for reducing infant mortality and otherwise promoting the health of
mothers and children, and 2) services for children who are crippled
or suffering from conditions leading to crippling." The original legislation required that there be an identifiable state agency and that
there be a state plan for the provision of maternal and child health
(MCH), and crippled childrens services (CCS). In most states the
same agency is responsible for MCH and CCS service and is usually
located in the State Health Department. In other states like Alabama, the CCS agency is in the Department of Education and has no
formal relationship to the MCH agency located in the State Health
Department.

Expansion of Social Security Act, Title V

In the 1960s Great Society public welfare expansion, additional
money was allocated under Title V of the Social Security Act for
special project grants to local institutions, usually in cities. This
"Program of Projects" included: 1) Maternal and Infant Care pro-

jects providing prenatal care and health services to eligible patients through the first year of life, 2) Children and Youth projects providing comprehensive health services to eligible children in a specific geographic area, 3) Dental health projects, 4) Neonatal Intensive Care projects, and 5) Family Planning projects. Funds were also set aside for training of personnel and for research related to MCH and CCS services. A number of training programs in such areas as genetic diseases, lung diseases, and mental retardation were established and, in many states, integrated into the health care delivery system. Later, in the 1970s, research and demonstration projects such as the Improved Pregnancy Outcome program, and the Improved Child Health program were used to improve the states' ability to deliver health services for poor women and children. These programs involved four or five year grants to states with the poorest child health statistics, and were aimed at increasing the states' capacity to provide maternal and child health services.

In addition to the Social Security Act, the Public Health Service Act was also used as a vehicle to initiate and fund a number of programs for children. These included project grants for the states or sub-state regions for sudden infant death syndrome (SIDS) information and counseling, grants for hemophilia treatment centers, grants for genetic disease testing and counseling programs, grants for sickle cell disease programs, and many others.

Appropriations were also made as part of the Social Security Act for a program which has come to be known as the Social Security Income Disabled Children's Program (SSI). The state agency which receives this funding is responsible for the administration of a state plan which provides free counseling, development of individual service plans, and referrals for disabled children under 16 years of age. In addition, this program provides medical, social, developmental, and rehabilitative services for disabled children under 7 years of age, and for those who have never attended public schools.

Public Health Service Act: Title X

Title X of the Public Health Service Act provides for statewide family planning programs. Title XX of the Social Security Act (Welfare) also provides that some funds be used for the provision of family planning services. As mentioned previously, Title V of the Social Security Act required (until 1981) that funds be used for family planning services.

Supplemental Food Program for Women, Infants, and Children (WIC)

In 1972 Congress enacted the Special Supplemental Food Program for Women, Infants, and Children, generally known as the WIC program. This program provides food supplements and nutrition education to pregnant women, lactating women, and children to age five. This program, unlike all those mentioned above, is not administered by the Department of Health and Human Services, but instead is a Department of Agriculture program administered by the Food and Nutrition Service. The WIC program is intimately linked with health care delivery, however, because recipients are required to show evidence of ongoing contact with medical services in order to maintain eligibility for participation in WIC.

Public Health Service Act: Section 330

Section 330 of the Public Health Service Act provided for the construction and maintenance of hundreds of community health centers throughout the United States. These programs attempted to provide community based primary care in both rural and urban health underserved areas. The National Health Service Corps represented an attempt to stock these centers and other programs in underserved areas with physicians and other health care providers.

Social Security Act: Title XIX-Medicaid Program

Despite the extensive number of programs described above and others not mentioned, it should be noted that the major funding program for the provision of health services to poor women and children is the Medicaid program. The importance of the Medicaid program to the funding of health care for indigent women and children, when compared to other programs, can be shown by the fact that nearly 80 percent of all public funds appropriated for the health care of pregnant women and children is expended through the Medicaid program. For this reason a brief description of Medicaid is in order.

Originally passed by Congress in the mid 1960s as Title XIX of the Social Security Act, the Medicaid program was conceived as a joint federal and state initiative to provide medical care for the country's poor. Based on the economic status of each state, the federal government contributes between 50 and approximately 80 percent of the total cost of this program. The state contributes the rest. There are some required services that must be supported and a number of optional services which the state can choose to provide. More important, the state has extensive options about who it will serve. States like Alabama, for example, chose to serve only those children eligible for welfare through the Aid to Dependent Children Program (ADC) of Title XX of the Social Security Act. In Alabama this program almost exclusively covers the children of poor, single women. Children of the married poor are not eligible for ADC and therefore not eligible for Medicaid as well. Many married, but poor pregnant women and their children in Alabama, and other states as well, therefore have no funding for their medical care.

Early Periodic Screening, Diagnosis, and Treatment (EPSDT)

One component of the Medicaid program aimed at children deserves special comment. The Early Periodic Screening, Diagnosis, and Treatment (EPSDT) program was made a required part of Medicaid in an attempt to encourage the states to provide preventive health care services to all Medicaid eligible children. This program requires the states to provide screening services with appropriate referral for medical treatment at regular intervals.

Utilization of Health Care Services by Poor Women

Because of the large variation in the need for government funded maternal and child health services from state to state, as well as the large variation in the ability of the states to provide those services, describing a model health care system for pregnant women and children is a difficult, if not impossible, task. In the best circumstances, an ideal child health system would be one in which all pregnant women and children, indigent or not, have equal access to the same high level of health care. Although this ideal has certainly not been realized, it is very important to remember that predominantly because of the programs described above, we are very much closer to achieving equal access to health care than we were 15 or 20 years ago. Numerous studies have shown that during that time there has been increased utilization of health care resources by poor pregnant women and poor children. In our own state of Alabama 20 years ago, 20 percent of all infants, and more than 40 percent of black infants were born outside of the hospital largely because their mothers were poor and could not afford the hospital or physicians' fees.[2] In the last year in Alabama less than 1 percent of all infants were born outside of the hospital, and the difference in utilization by race was small. The programs described above can claim most the credit for the improved access to health care for poor and minority women and children.

This is not to say that health care for the poor is always available, attainable, or of satisfactory quality. Despite these programs, poor children are less likely to be immunized, less likely to be seen for the very important anticipatory guidance and preventive health services, and are often refused care in the private medical care system. Frequently, they receive care in a fragmented and piecemeal fashion. Poor women receive less than half the number of prenatal visits of middle class women, and black women receive less than half the prenatal visits of white women. For these reasons, among others, poor and black infant mortality rates are generally twice those of white or middle class infants.[3]

LOCAL IMPLEMENTATION OF FEDERAL PROGRAMS

Eligibility Influences

Before one can talk about what the ideal system must look like, some of the problems inherent in the multiple federally funded program approach should be discussed. Most obvious is the fact that all the federal programs providing funds for the health care of children have different rules and regulations, and very often different criteria for admission to the program. Therefore a child may fit the criteria for the WIC program, but may not be eligible for the Maternal and Child Health program, both of which may be operated within the same county health department. Children may be eligible for Crippled Children's Services but not the WIC program, etc.

Geographic Problems

Another common problem is that the programs themselves may not be located in close geographical proximity. Even if they are, these programs often meet at different times. In many cases even if the clinics are held in the same building, at the same hours of the same day, and they are eligible for all services, poor pregnant women, or women with young children are often confronted with a seemingly endless series of lines, waiting periods, and paperwork. For these and other reasons, even when the potential resources are apparently available to provide appropriate health care, because of the fragmentation in the health service delivery system, the care that poor women and children receive is frequently less than optimal.

Availability of Resources

Unfortunately, the resources to provide health care for poor children are often not available. The provision of health services to children requires that there be a capacity to deliver those services. Very simply, there must be, within a reasonable and accessible distance, a sufficient number of medical care providers so that health care services can be rendered. Despite the seeming overabundance of physicians nationally, many inner-cities as well as rural areas have severe health manpower shortages. Even if there are sufficient providers, these providers must be willing to provide health care to poor women and children. All too often they are not, and in many instances federal subsidization of care through the Medicaid program has not alleviated this problem. Many physicians, either because of low payment, excessive paper work, or philosophical disagreement, refuse to provide medical care to eligible pregnant women and children funded by the Medicaid program.

In addition to providing funding through Medicaid program, the intent of much of the federal legislation from the 1960s to about 1980 was aimed at increasing the capacity of the medical care system to provide health care, especially for poor women and children. Initiatives, especially of the Title V program, such as the Maternal and Infant Care projects, the Children and Youth projects, the dental projects, etc., were really attempts at capacity building. The federally funded community health centers which became so prevalent during the late 1970s were another attempt to increase the capacity to provide health care using federal funds. The federally funded family planning program was another capacity building program. The National Health Service Corps, a program which placed physicians and other providers in health underserved areas, was still another attempt along these lines. Federal rules and regulations required the Medicaid program, using both state and federal funds, to reimburse the other federal programs for services provided to indigent patients, transferring funds from a payment program to the "capacity" building programs.

Organization of Services

By 1980, with the clinical space and providers available through the capacity building programs, and with funding through the Medicaid program, it appeared that there were nearly sufficient resources both in capacity and funds, to provide reasonable health care to most of the nation's poor women and children. The problem in 1980 seemed more organizational in nature than one either of capacity or funding. Fragmentation in the delivery of services to the poor, primarily because of conflicting federal rules and regulations, compounded at the state and local level by jurisdictional disputes seemed to be the major problem. In 1980, efforts were under way at all levels of government to solve these problems. As an example, the Congressional Select Panel for Child Health was established to evaluate existing services to children and to recommend changes that could lead to improvement in service delivery and health status.[4]

CHILD HEALTH BLOCK GRANTS

By 1982, however, the situation had changed radically. First, there was a real attempt to reduce some of the fragmentation described above by combining programs into "block grants," and removing some of the conflicting regulations. A Maternal and Child Health Block Grant was created, combining 6 of the programs mentioned above (MCH, CCS, Genetics, SIDS, Sickle Cell, and SSI). Many of the regulations were eliminated. Had this alone been done, and the money allocated to the states in one package rather than multiple small packages, with some of the conflicting rules and regulations attending each program eliminated, some of the fragmentation described above could, indeed, have been resolved. Greater efficiency and better health care would likely have been the result.

However, another component of the "block grant" legislation was to reduce the federal oversight of health care programs affecting women and children. While the effects of this reduced federal presence is unknown, in many instances, it assured that the funds were used appropriately to provide health services to women and children in need. Perhaps one effect of this reduced federal presence will be the less appropriate use of funds for the health care of women and children. Of course, it can be argued that because the state and local governments are closer to the people that the money will be better spent as local people make more of the decisions. The results from this experiment in health care delivery are not yet available.

The results may, in fact, never be available. With the "block grant" legislation there came a very clear indication from the Reagan Administration that it was not interested in either obtaining information about state needs in the area of maternal and child health, or in collecting data about the effectiveness of state and local MCH programs. Many years' efforts at collecting maternal and child health care statistics seem now to be purposefully neglected. It is as if the federal government under this administration is saying "if we do not know what the needs are, then no one can ask for help to solve them. The less that is known about the health of women and children, the better."

The major effect of the Reagan administration's efforts has been in the area of funding. Besides being placed into the "block grant," over the last 2 years many maternal and child health programs have had funding reductions approaching 40 percent. With an annual inflation rate during that time of 10 percent or more, the Maternal and Child Health Programs, The Crippled Children's Program, Family Planning, Sudden Infant Death Syndrome, The Disabled Children's Program, etc., have all experienced massive reductions in their ability to provide services for poor women and children. It is this reduction in funds for maternal and child health in a period of recession when state resources are diminishing as well, which is severely limiting the availability of health care services for poor women and children. Very simply, the capacity which these programs once had to provide services is no longer present. In Alabama, because of the reduction in funds, the state Maternal and Child Health Program no longer can provide dental services, nutrition services, or social work services, and has sharply reduced its health education program. Several county health departments that once provided prenatal and child care no longer have the capacity to do so.

Medicaid funding reductions are also limiting access to care, as state after state is reducing the number of allowable hospital days, eliminating optional services, and restricting the number of eligibles. Many institutions that provide care to Medicaid funded women and children are facing severe fiscal crises. If the proposed cuts in the Medicaid budget for the 1983 fiscal year are enacted, funding for vital health services for pregnant women and children will be severely restricted.

THE MODEL SYSTEM

A model health care system for pregnant women and children should have several features (see Table 1). First, especially for poor women and children, health care should be freely accessible and not restricted because of financial considerations. Second, the health care should be logistically attainable, and not so temporally or geographically scattered as to be realistically unattainable. The health care that is available should emphasize screening and preventive education, but should be connected to a system of secondary and tertiary care so that the sickest pregnant women and their children will receive a level of care commensurate with their needs.

Given the current political realities, it is unlikely that in the near future there will be a single funding source that will enable all women and children, rich and poor, to receive their care through the private medical system.[5] Therefore, the "model system" that we will describe will be based on currently funded programs. We will assume that, for the most part, poor women and children will receive their health care through local agencies funded by the pro-

TABLE 1. Home Health Care: A Model System for Maternal and Child Health.

ONE AGENCY PROVIDES ALL THE HEALTH CARE FOR POOR PREGNANT
WOMEN AND CHILDREN

1. Health care is freely accessible regardless of financial
   consideration.

2. Home Health Care is geographically situated so as to be
   within close proximity to their home.

3. Screening and Prevention Treatment Programs are connected
   to secondary and tertiary care systems.

4. There is a capacity to provide many types of health-related
   services.

5. A single set of standards is adopted by appropriate local
   consumers and providers.

6. The fragmentation of services is eliminated.

7. A referral system is used for medical problems needing
   secondary and tertiary care.

grams already described. We should emphasize that even though this is to be a "model system," in fact, we are describing a two tiered system in which middle-class patients are more likely to use a private physician while patients without funds will depend on the resources of the federally funded programs.

From the discussions above, it should be obvious that the primary need is one of capacity sufficient to care for all eligible patients within a specific goegraphic area. This capacity, of necessity, will be derived from a number of sources, their identity depending on the local situation. Whenever possible this capacity should involve a combination of private practicing physicians, health departments, community health centers, hospital based health care programs, and other agencies capable of providing health care to women and children. Obviously in those areas where there is no capacity to provide medical services, some combination of federal and state resources should be used to develop that capacity.

The next consideration should be one of standards. While it is unlikely that a single medical care delivery system can be created, it should be feasible to provide care under a single set of standards. Wherever the care is received, whether in the private sector or though a public agency, these standards should be met. In our "model system," at the local level, an appropriate group of consumers and providers would define the contents of appropriate health care for pregnant women and children in that geographic area, and should be able to set minimal standards for that care.

The major problem to overcome after the capacity to deliver services is assured, is to reduce the fragmentation inherent in the multiple federal program approach. Pregnant women or children deemed eligible for one federal maternal and child health program, should be eligible for all appropriate maternal and child health programs. Every attempt should be made to enable each child to receive all health care services in a single location under the auspices of a single (although multiply funded) local program. Therefore, if a health department has customarily provided WIC services while a nearby community health center has been providing routine anticipatory guidance services, a restructuring should take place so that individual children will receive all their health care under the auspices of one agency. The aim of all those in authority at the federal, state, and local levels of government should be directed toward this end. Therefore, there should be one institution which assumes responsibility for the pregnant woman's or child's health care. For example, for children, this institution should be responsible for the child's immunizations, for anticipatory guidance on a routine schedule, for all appropriate screening examinations, and for routine acute medical care as well. In other words, the child should be assured a "health care home," as recommended by the American Academy of Pediatrics. The staff of this "home," if not a private physician's office, may optimally include not only traditional health care providers such as physicians and nurses, but also dentists, dental technicians, social workers, nutrition specialists, and health educators.

This is not to say that we would expect a local agency such as a health department or a community health center to provide all levels of medical care. The model system, therefore, would have another major component in addition to providing basic health care. This component would be a very structured and appropriate referral system for specific medical problems. The model health care system, therefore, would have written agreements between the local agency and various kinds of more specialized secondary and tertiary institutions. For example, pregnant women who became ill, or seemed likely to have a premature delivery, would be referred to an appropriate high risk obstetrical unit. Children with crippling diseases would be referred through appropriate channels to a hospital or crippled children's agency where the appropriate medical care would be available. In other words, the resources from all federally funded Maternal and Child Health programs, and the available state and local resources would be pooled to provide a health care system based on the needs of the pregnant women and children they are meant to serve, not to provide services based on the needs of the individual federally funded programs.

As mentioned above, the key to this system is a "health care home" for each child. This concept requires that a single physician or group of physicians in private practice, or a single agency such as the health department or a community health center, be given the responsibility for insuring the appropriate health care for each child. The "health care home" will be responsible for providing a specific set of services and, when indicated, responsible for referring for other services. If every pregnant woman and child in a geographic area had a "health care home," much of the fragmentation resulting in so much of the poor health care currently provided for poor pregnant women and children would be eliminated.

It should be obvious from the discussions above that it is not possible to describe exactly how this concept will work in any particular location. Clearly, a scheme of organization which works well for Navaho children in Arizona may be very different from that which will work for black children in the South Bronx. What works in one county in Alabama will not work in another. Nevertheless, if we can all remember that the goal of all the federally funded and state and locally administered programs is to provide health care services to children not otherwise receiving them, then it should be obvious that reduction in fragmentation in the delivery system is an absolute necessity. Those agencies able and willing to provide a health care home for pregnant women and children should be the recipients of the funds available. Those agencies that cannot or will not assume this responsibility, and continue to provide only fragments of the health care required should not be funded.

In summary, the model health care system for children described above has as major features a reduction in fragmentation of services and the provision of a "health care home." There are a number of areas in the United States in which poor children are served by agencies striving to achieve these goals. For example, the Jefferson County, Alabama, Health Department has been successfully consolidating its programs for mothers and children, has assumed the role of "health care home" for many of its patients, and is working closely with the University Medical Center to provide a coordinated system of specialized care for those in need. Using computers, they have introduced a common medical record system. The North Carolina Health Department, in conjunction with the North Carolina Academy of Pediatrics, has pioneered the "health care home" concept for poor children. Mississippi and South Carolina have both made substantial progress in consolidating maternity and child health services. Other examples of reduced fragmentation resulting in improved health care, cited in a report being prepared by the Institute of Medicine, include public health agencies in West Palm Beach, Florida; Denver, Colorado; Seattle, Washington; and Boston, Massachusetts. Nevertheless in virtually every area of the United States, women and children are poorly served because of the continued fragmentation of health services and the absence of a specific health care advocate. We can only hope that the recent severe federal funding reductions can be restored so that throughout the United States progress toward our model system can be continued.

REFERENCES

1. Goldenberg, R. L., Humphrey, J. L., Hale, C. B., Wayne, J. B. Neonatal Mortality in Alabama 1940-1980. An Analysis of Birthweight and Race Specific Neonatal Mortality Rates. *Am J. Obstet Gynec.* In Press.

2. Houde, J., Humphrey, J. L., Boyd, B. W., Goldenberg, R. L. Out of Hospital Deliveries in Alabama, 1940-1980. *J. Med Assoc St of Al.,* 52:20, 1982.

3. Goldenberg, R. L. Maternal and Child Health in Alabama. *J Med Assoc State Ala,* 13, March 1979.

4. The Report of the Select Panel for the Promotion of Child Health: Better Health For Our Children: A National Strategy. The U.S. Department of Health and Human Services. DHHS Publication No. 7955071.

5. Lazarus, W. How states can use limited health resources for children and mothers most effectively-Presented at the Conference on State Action to Improve Maternal and Child Health, Washington, D.C., May 5-7, 1982.

EDUCATION ISSUES

Introduction

Bette Everett Hamilton, PhD
Barbara A. Bush, JD

Since 1965, the federal role in education had evolved out of concern for children with special educational needs and the inability or unwillingness of states and LEAs (Local Education Agencies) to provide for those needs without federal resources and specific programs. From 1965 to 1982, Title I of the Elementary and Secondary Education Act (ESEA) was the funding source for these children, but weathered a stormy history including major program abuses in the early years when many LEAs used Title I funds as general aid, providing no supplemental benefit to eligible participants.[1]

During these 17 years, the Title I law and regulations were amended nine times. Each time, refinements were made to better ensure educational benefits for eligible children while fostering the concomitant learning of federal and state bureaucrats in working with LEAs. Ironically, Title I had become a dramatically successful federal education program, even by the standards of the Reagan Administration, when it was abolished in 1981. Recent national evaluations of educational progress found, for example, that achievement gains were the greatest for black pre-adolescents in those very same districts that received high Title I allocations.[2]

On August 13, 1981, President Reagan signed into law the

Bette Everett Hamilton is Education Director, Children's Defense Fund and Barbara A. Bush is Senior Attorney, Children's Defense Fund, 1520 New Hampshire Ave., NW., Washington, D.C. 20036.

Education Consolidation and Improvement Act, ECIA. The ECIA can be viewed as the first step in accomplishing the Reagan Administration's mandate to substantially reduce the federal role in education and devolve full responsibility for education back to the states and local governments.

Chapter I replaced Title I of the ESEA, the cornerstone federal program that aided low-resource school districts in education disadvantaged children who were behind their peers in school achievement. The fundamental purpose of Chapter I remains the same as that of Title I:

> to continue to provide financial assistance to state and local educational agencies to meet the special needs of educationally deprived children" but with the caveat. . . to do so in a manner which will eliminate burdensome, unnecessary, and unproductive paperwork and free the schools of unnecessary Federal supervision, direction, and control.[3]

Under Chapter I, money will continue to flow to LEAs for the provision of compensatory education to educationally disadvantaged children, but due to the non-existence of accountability provisions, no federal oversight, and marginal state monitoring and enforcement, the educational benefit to eligible children will depend on the goodwill, honesty, and commitment of local school officials. With retrenchment of the federal role in education, closer state and local monitoring of school policy and practice is critical to ensure that the genuine "welfare" of all children is being served nationally.

REFERENCES

1. See Martin, Ruby, & McClure. *Title I of ESEA: Is It Helping Poor Children?* Washington, D.C.: Washington Research Project of the Children's Defense Fund, and NAACP Legal Defense and Educational Fund, Inc., 1969 See Kirst & Jung. The utility of a longitudinal approach in assessing implementation: A thirteen year view of Title I ESEA. *Education Evaluation and Policy Analysis,* Sept. 1980.

2. Roy Forbes. *National Assessment of Educational Progress,* Denver: Education Commission of the States, April 1981.

3. (Sec. 552 Chapter I ECIA, P. L. 97-35, Title V, Subtitle D).

Policy:
From Title I to Chapter I:
Step I Towards New Federalism

Bette Everett Hamilton, PhD
Barbara A. Bush, JD

ABSTRACT. On August 13, 1981, President Reagan signed into law the Education Consolidation and Improvement Act (ECIA). Chapter I of the new law replaced Title I of the Elementary and Secondary Education Act of 1965, a program designed to provide remedial educational services to educationally deprived children in low-income school districts. The authors characterize Chapter I as "a first step in accomplishing the Reagan Administration's mandate to substantially reduce the federal role in education and devolve full responsibility for education back to the states and local governments."

The authors describe how the program changes, combined with the lack of clarity and detailed guidance in the new statute, significantly diminishes the federal role in compensatory education and gives almost complete discretion to local school officials in the selection of the schools and children to be served by the program, and in its design, implementation and evaluation. They foresee in these changes an enhanced potential for abuse in implementation of the program and serious legal and policy conflicts.

To illustrate the potential for inconsistent interpretations of the statutory requirements by the various states, the authors describe the different approaches to implementing the new law being taken in 4 states: Connecticut, Arizona, New York, and Mississippi. They conclude that, in the absence of a clear national commitment to eradicating the link between poverty and educational deprivation, Chapter I cannot guarantee that the poorest and most educationally needy children will be served by the federal program. Serving these children will now be a matter of state and local option and commitment.

MAJOR STATUTORY AND POLICY CHANGES

Despite Congress' declaration that Chapter I's purposes are the same as those of Title I, Chapter I is *not* Title I (see Table I). The new statute repeals or substantially modifies many of the detailed provisions of Title I which were designed to ensure the effectiveness of the program, accountability on the part of SEAs and LEAs, and that program funds were directed towards achieving Congressionally-sanctioned purposes. Some of the differences between Title I

TABLE 1. Differences between Title I and Chapter I

	TITLE I	CHAPTER I
Targeting Funds	Eligible children were selected on basis of relative education deprivation. Priority given to most educationally deprived	Unspecified part of funds for all low-income children. No priority given to children with greatest need for educational assistance.
Fiscal Requirements	Insured federal, state, and local funds would be used for educationally deprived. Documentation of "comparability".	Insures only federal funds used for educationally deprived. LEAs now determine expenditure of local funds No documentation of "comparability". LEA required to file "comparability" with SEA only.
Program Design, Implementation, & Evaluation	Encouraged development of individualized eduation plans (IEP). Provided for parents to be actively involved in program development etc. Program evaluation conducted in accordance with standardized evaluation models.	Dispenses provision for development of IEPs. Programs are designed & implemented "in consultation" with parents & teachers. Program evaluation does not have to be conducted in accordance with standardized evaluation models.
Accountability	SEA responsible for LEA compliance to Title I. Department of Education had legal authority over SEA and LEA	SEAs have limited authority over LEAs. Department of Education does not have legal authority over SEAs & LEAs.

and Chapter I are explained under the following four primary areas: targeting of funds; fiscal requirements; program design, implementation, evaluation; and accountability.

Targeting of Funds

Title I was predicated on the high correlation between poverty and educational deprivation. Title I also acknowledged that schools in attendance areas having the largest concentrations of low-income children would be the least financially able to provide supplemental educational services with their own local resources. Thus, in order to ensure that limited federal education funds were concentrated only on educationally deprived children in low-income attendance areas, Title I utilized a funding formula which allocated funds both to and within school districts based on counts of low-income children. It required school districts to rank their schools in order of poverty, and to give priority in the selection of project schools to the poorest. Once monies reached these schools, however, eligible children were selected on the basis of relative educational deprivation, with the most educationally deprived children receiving priority.

Chapter I continues this allocation formula, but does not specify how or what criteria school districts are to use to identify those school attendance areas having the highest concentrations of low-income children nor require that the poorest attendance areas be given priority in selection as project sites. Chapter I also permits LEAs to use some unspecified part of their funds to provide services for *all* low-income children within the school district. Although school districts must still conduct annual needs assessments of eligible attendance areas to identify eligible children, children with the greatest need for educational assistance need not be given priority or selected at all for participation in the program. These substantive changes in the Chapter I Statute gives LEAs almost complete discretion to determine which schools and which children will participate in the program. How school districts will exercise this discretion in selecting project areas and children to participate in Chapter I projects remains to be seen.

Even with Title I's targeting provisions and clear Congressional mandate in place, compliance was not always guaranteed. Therefore, with the current pressures of insufficient funds and consequent impossibility of serving all eligible children, targeting requirements are more necessary if children, who are furthest behind their peers in school, are to receive the intended benefits of the program.

There is no evidence in the legislative history of Chapter I to suggest that Congress has retreated from this long-held position. However, there does appear to be some tension between Congress' declaration that the purposes of Title I are continued in Chapter I and its simultaneous relaxation of Title I targeting provisions. Congress' dilution of the targeting provisions raises serious legal and policy questions concerning the intended parameters of SEA and LEA discretion, and whether the poorest schools and the most educationally needy children will indeed be served.

Fiscal Requirements

Title I contained a number of provisions designed to ensure the supplemental nature of the federal program. For example, the *Comparability* requirement protected children being served by the federal program from being penalized by the reduction of state and local educational services made available to them. The *Supplement Not Supplant* provision required that federal funds be used to augment rather than to replace state and locally-financed educational services, and state and local agencies were required to at least maintain level funding for general education from year to year (*Maintenance of Effort*). Together, these provisions helped to ensure not only that educationally deprived children received federal compensatory services, but also that they received their fair share of state and locally-funded services.

Under Chapter I, these fiscal accountability requirements are continued, but somewhat relaxed. LEAs are still required to use Chapter I funds to supplement, and not supplant funds being made available from other non-federal sources for the education of children participating in Chapter I programs. However, for purposes of determining compliance with this provision, Chapter I allows LEAs to discount state and local funds expended for compensatory education. Thus, state compensatory education funds are freed-up to serve more non-poor schools and children.

Although Title I required school districts to maintain expenditures for public education at 100 percent of the prior year's level as a condition of receipt of federal funds, the supplementary effect of federal funds was eroded with the inflation index, since there was no requirement that the "maintenance of effort" be adjusted for inflation. Chapter I considerably accelerates this downward spiral by requiring only that 90 percent of the previous year's fiscal effort be maintained in order for an LEA to receive its full allocation of Chapter I funds. An LEA which fails to meet this maintenance of effort requirement will have its Chapter I funds reduced proportionately, compared to a complete cut-off of funds in the past under Title I.

Finally, under Title I, school districts were required to document "comparability" i.e., their compliance with the statutory mandate to provide roughly the same level of services to children in Title I project schools as to those in non-Title I schools. This was generally measured in terms of relative teacher-pupil ratios, expenditures per pupil, teacher qualifications, teacher salaries, curricula, and materials provided in project and non-project schools. The comparability requirement proved to be a significant factor in spurring school districts to equalize the distribution of state and local resources to poor, often largely minority, school attendance areas.

Chapter I reduces the comparability requirement to a set of written assertions. The LEA must only have on file with its State Education Agency (SEA) a written assurance that it has established (a) a district-wide salary schedule; (b) a *policy* to ensure equivalence among schools and teachers, administrators and auxiliary personnel; and (c) a *policy* to ensure equivalence among schools in the provision of curriculum materials and instructional supplies. No special documentation is required to show that the LEA has in fact implemented these policies.

Program Design, Implementation, and Evaluation

LEAs had considerable flexibility under Title I as to program design. Certain Title I constraints on this otherwise substantial discretion of state and local agencies were designed by Congress to promote program effectiveness. For example, Title I required LEAs, as a part of their annual needs assessment, to determine the particular special educational needs of participating children with sufficient specificity to ensure concentration on those needs. Programs were also required to be of sufficient size, scope and quality to give reasonable promise of substantial progress toward meeting the identified needs of the children served. Moreover, the Title I statute encouraged the development of individualized education plans (IEPs) for each educationally deprived child, as a further means of ensuring that the particular educational needs of each participating child were met by the program. Chapter I still requires LEAs to concentrate program resources on the educational needs of children served, but it dispenses with the Title I provision suggesting the development of IEPs, and encourages the treatment of children in the aggregate.

Title I recognized that parents could play an important role both in the education of their children and in safeguarding the quality of the program. LEAs were required to establish parent advisory councils, generally at both the school district and individual project levels. These parent advisory councils had responsibility for advising school districts on the development, implementation, and evaluation of Title I projects. Parents were guaranteed access to program documents and records pertinent to the operation of local projects and were provided training necessary for their meaningful involvement in the program.

In contrast, Chapter I mandates only that programs be designed and implemented "in consultation" with parents (and teachers) of children served by the program. It does not require the establishment or maintenance of formal parent advisory councils, does not specify what degree of interaction or involvement of parents is required by the term "consult," and does not guarantee parents access to project records and documents.

Under Chapter I, program evaluations no longer have to be conducted in accordance with standardized evaluation models. Thus, local project data may not be comparable, and it will therefore be impossible for any accurate assessment of the program's effectiveness to be done on the national level.

Accountability

Title I established a number of "check points" to hold LEAs accountable for complying with the law. First, complaint procedures and other mechanisms existed for parents and interested members of the public to oversee local projects. Second, SEAs were vested by statute with substantial monitoring, oversight, rulemaking, and enforcement authority. SEAs were responsible for providing technical assistance to LEAs as well as guidance on the design and implementation of local projects through appropriate regulations. SEAs were also charged with reviewing LEA project evaluations, requiring LEAs to submit periodic reports, and for hearing appeals of complaints initiated at the LEA level. They also had the authority to audit local projects and withhold LEA funds where maintenance of effort, supplement-not-supplant, comparability, or other program requirements were not satisfied. Third, the federal Department of Education had the ultimate oversight responsibility and authority for issuing binding interpretations of the statute and enforcing compliance with its provisions.

Chapter I, on the other hand, makes SEAs almost entirely responsible for ensuring LEA compliance with the law. Yet, SEAs have explicit authority under the statute only for approving LEA applications and reducing allocations or granting waivers (under limited circumstances) to LEAs who fail to meet maintenance of efforts requirements. Chapter I requires LEAs to "keep such records and provide such information to the SEA as may be required for fiscal audit and program evaluation" (consistent with the responsibilities of the SEA), but does not explicitly confer authority on SEAs to audit, evaluate, or to issue rules specifying what records are to be kept, or with what frequency they are to be submitted by LEAs.[1]

Chapter I specifically limits the Department of Education to issuing only such rules as are: (a) related to the Secretary's discharge of duties specifically assigned by the statute; (b) related to proper fiscal accounting for Chapter I funds; and (c) deemed necessary to ensure compliance with specific Chapter I assurances and requirements. The Secretary is explicitly prohibited from issuing regulations on "all other matters relating to the details of planning, developing, implementing and evaluating programs and projects by State and local education agencies."

Moreover, general provisions of the ECIA provide that any regulations issued by the Secretary to implement the Chapter I (and Chapter II) program shall not have the force of law. As a legal consequence, Departmental regulations under Chapter I will not be entitled to the same deference by the Courts as were Title I regulations and thus, even if promulgated, will be more difficult to enforce. In the meantime, SEAs and LEAs are left to implement the Chapter I program which became effective on October 1, 1982 with no guidance and almost unlimited discretion.

REFERENCE

1. A separate law, the General Education Provisions Act (GEPA) which applies to all programs under the administrative authority of the Secretary of Education, unless specifically made inapplicable by another statute, would have provided the enforcement authority

necessary for SEAs to carry out their responsibilities under Chapter I. In addition, GEPA would have forced LEA compliance with applicable civil rights laws, and granted Congress "veto" authority over Departmental regulations. However, it is unclear which sections of GEPA specifically apply to the ECIA. In final regulations promulgated on July 12, 1982, the Department of Education alleged that only those sections of GEPA that govern fiscal accounting and the carry-over of funds apply to Chapter I (and Chapter II.) Ironically, Congress subsequently vetoed the regulations, using its power under GEPA (that the Department alleged did not apply). The issue may ultimately be decided by the courts.

Practice:
State Implementation of Chapter I

Bette Everett Hamilton, PhD
Barbara A. Bush, JD

ABSTRACT. The flexibility with which the states have interpreted and implemented the ECIA is illustrated in examples drawn from four regions of the United States.

Some SEAs and LEAs will continue to administer their Chapter I programs in much the same manner as Title I. Others will allow Chapter I to become what Title I was in the early years, a more or less general aid program with little educational benefit to children. Title I was a "child-oriented" program with parental guarantees; Chapter I is a program for education agencies, with the prohibition against "overly prescriptive regulations and administrative burdens."

The 50 states have developed 50 different interpretations of the Chapter I program and what roles state and local educational agencies should play in the implementation process. Some states, like Connecticut, Massachusetts, and Rhode Island have encouraged a strong state agency lead and the issuance of state guidance which reinstates many of Title I's requirements. Massachusetts wanted to go so far as to *require* that LEAs continue their former parent advisory councils (PAC)s, but was persuaded by Washington that the statute made PACs an LEA option.

Other states have given some guidance in certain areas of the law, but leave other areas deliberately vague. Some states even encourage LEAs to use Chapter I funds in legally questionable ways. Finally, those states with a long history of weak state educational agencies give almost total discretion to LEAs and ask only for minimal "check-off" reports to placate federal auditors. These different state operating styles are exemplified by four cases: Connecticut, Arizona, New York, and Mississippi.

CONNECTICUT

Connecticut's State Education Department (CSED) has provided extensive guidance to its LEAs on how to implement Chapter I programs.[1] LEAs are required to demonstrate to CSED that they are complying with state interpretations of federal requirements. For instance, Connecticut has reinstated former Title I (or very similar) provisions for all Chapter I projects in the following areas:

- Excess Cost (Supplement not Supplant)
- Comparability reporting and record keeping
- State (CSED) monitoring of LEAs for compliance
- Right of CSED to withhold Chapter I funds to LEAs for non-compliance
- Allowing LEAs to by-pass higher ranked schools if other comparable programs are in place (not specifically carried over by statute)
- Access to information requirements for parents and the general public (including Chapter I application; reports on monitoring, evaluation and audit; and any other records and documents pertinent to the operation of Chapter I.)
- Continued selection of children with greatest need for compensatory education
- Complaint procedures in place at LEA, with right of appeal to CSED

In addition, because Chapter I makes some former Title I requirements (e.g., parent advisory councils) optional, the CSED *strongly recommends,* but does not require, that LEAs retain their parent advisory councils and encourages the use of Chapter I funds for parent training. CSED also recommends continued use of standardized evaluation models. Regulating beyond Title I and Chapter I requirements, Connecticut's state agency even restricts program design by requiring LEAs to limit Chapter I "pull-out" programs[2] to no more than 20 percent of the total instructional time a child spends in class.

ARIZONA

Arizona's guidance to its LEAs is less comprehensive than Connecticut's but has many of the same features.[3] In its Chapter I guidance, the Arizona Department of Education argues for a continuation of the Title I format.

> Although the district is not required to submit detailed plans for prior Department approval it is important to remember that the district MUST MAINTAIN ADEQUATE DOCUMENTATION OF PROJECT COMPONENTS AND ACTIVITIES for local dissemination, project audit and monitoring, and for evaluation purposes. It is suggested that the simplest means to develop and maintain this documentation is to use or adapt the present Title I format in the various accountability areas.

In addition, Arizona requires not only assurances from LEAs that they will comply with Chapter I provisions but also *documentation* that they are in compliance with the state interpretations in the following areas:

- Needs Assessment (Maintaining a brief description of district needs assessment plans and activities, dated record of major activities, summaries of key data used in prioritization of needs, and the final list of priorities by school.)
- target school selection (ranking of schools)
- participant selection ("The most deficient students are always selected first.")
- program design (size, scope and quality; and supplement not supplant)
- parent and teacher consultation

Arizona gives LEAs specific criteria to follow in targeting funds and schools, selecting students and developing program design. In addition to recommending parent advisory councils, Arizona suggests that consultation activities might include "workshops, orientation meetings, surveys, and individual conferences. . . ."

NEW YORK

New York is a rather unique case. Although it has issued considerable guidance to LEAs, most of its interpretations of Chapter I requirements dilute federal standards to comply with State policies and practices.[4] New York State has long had its own compensatory education program, Pupils with Special Educational Needs (PSEN). PSEN differs from Title I (and now Chapter I), in that all academically deficient students (including limited English proficient students and non-educationally deprived handicapped children, i.e., those with learning disabilities), are eligible to participate in the program regardless of the income level of their school attendance areas. Title I also required more concentration of resources on eligible students, smaller class sizes and more attention, comparability of state and local programs within LEAs, and considerable parent involvement.

New York has sought to combine Chapter I with PSEN, by allowing LEAs to allocate Chapter I funds to any school attendance area (including those wealthier than the district's average) provided schools in the poorer attendance areas are served by PSEN or some other program. The programs would thus be interchangeable, although the federal program technically should have more restrictions and protections. New York State's guidance to LEAs bars the use of all "pull-out" programs, which will mean that Chapter I "projects" will have to be incorporated into the regular classroom. (It also may mean that the eligible children are only getting what they would have received in the regular classroom without Chapter I, in violation of the supplement-not-supplant provisions.)

In addition, the New York State Education Department has sought permission from the U.S. Department of Education to:[5]

- carry out "schoolwide projects" with Chapter I funds whenever a majority (51%) of pupils enrolled in a school are from low-income families;
- waive all requirements of Chapter I "when an LEA wishes to pool its local, state compensatory education, and Chapter I resources for remedial instruction";
- include handicapped children and limited English proficient children under the rubric of educationally deprived children when computing costs for comparability reporting.

Such practices, if allowed by the federal government, will have the effect of reducing Chapter I to general aid.

MISSISSIPPI

Mississippi's guidance to LEAs is minimal, but it does not openly violate the Chapter I law.[6] The LEA must submit an application of assurances (a series of check-offs) to the SEA. Statutory language is reiterated in the application without any interpretation of meaning by the SEA. The LEA is required to give a brief description of program thrust (activities, grade levels, number of children, instructional strategies,) and a brief description of how the program will be designed and implemented in consultation with parents and teachers. The LEA must include reporting forms to indicate how Chapter I money is spent and how evaluations are conducted.

While all of the above information must be on file with the SEA, the state agency gives LEAs no guidance as to: the targeting of resources and services on attendance areas and schools; needs assessment and the selection of children; program design; supplement not supplant requirements; or parent consultation. In Mississippi, it seems that the interpretation of all these program areas are now totally the prerogative of local school officials.

REFERENCES

1. See "Handbook for Programs Funded Under Chapter I of the Education Consolidation and Improvement Act of 1981," Connecticut State Department of Education, May 1982, mimeo.

2. Pull-out programs provide remedial instruction for eligible children outside the regular classroom. They are controversial because although they provide concentrated program services and allow for easy audits, they also stigmatize children by placing them in low-ability tracks.

3. "Chapter I, ECIA Application Guidelines," Arizona Department of Education, Spring, 1982, mimeo.

4. See "Memorandum to District Superintendents of Public and Nonpublic Schools, and ECIA Chapter I/PSEN Coordinators," from Maria Ramirez, Assistant Commissioner, Subject: The Comprehensive Plan for Remediation and Application for ECIA Chapter I and PSEN funds for School Year 1982-83, New York State Department of Education, May, 1982, mimeo.

5. See Letter to Secretary T. H. Bell, from Gordon M. Ambach, Commissioner of Education, State of New York, May 21, 1982.

6. "LEA Application for Grant to Meet the Special Educational Needs of Educationally Deprived Children Under Chapter I of the Education Consolidation and Improvement Act of 1981," Mississippi Department of Education," July 1, 1982, mimeo.

Introduction

Joanne Selinske, MS

In the past two decades, several events have directed attention to the enormous human and economic costs to society of child abuse and neglect, and to prompte legislation mandating the reporting of, and public intervention in cases of child maltreatment. The 1960 Golden Anniversary White House Conference on Children and Youth, recommended that states enact legislation authorizing communities to delegate responsibility for receiving and responding to reports of child abuse and neglect to a specific social agency. Shortly thereafter, Congress passed the 1962 amendments to the Social Security Act, requiring states to develop plans to extend child welfare services, including protective services, to all their political subdivisions. In the same year, Kempe's formal identification of the "battered child syndrome" mobilized concern within the medical community. Shortly after the reporting by Dr. Kempe of the findings of his national survey, the Children's Bureau of the U.S. Department of Health, Education and Welfare (DHEW) held a conference on the battered child (Kadushin, 1980). By 1967, fifty states, the District of Columbia, and the Virgin Islands had adopted reporting legislation, providing a foundation for efforts to ameliorate the problem of child maltreatment.

Today, the apparent need for this public response is well docu-

---

Joanne Selinske, is affiliated with Marriage and Family Counseling/Family Studies. Consultant to the American Bar Association's National Legal Resource Center for Child Advocacy and Protection, 1800 M Street, N.W., Washington, D. C. 20036.

55

mented. In 1980 alone, state child protective service agencies received more than 788,000 reports of child maltreatment (The American Humane Association, 1981-Refer Notes). Compared to 1976, this represents a reporting increase of 91%.

As reports of child abuse and neglect has increased, the duties of the state and local agencies providing child protective services has broadened. It became the full-time responsibility of the child protective agencies to ensure the prompt investigation of reports, and provide for the immediate protection of abused and neglected children.

In 1974, Congress responded to the growing concern for the safety and well-being of America's children with the passage of P.L. 93-247. The law created the National Center on Child Abuse and Neglect (NCCAN), within DHEW, to catalize efforts to identify, prevent, and to treat child abuse and neglect through research, demonstration and information dissemination. The Act was not designed to augment federal service dollars allocated to protective services from Title XX funds, but offered states financial incentives to reform child abuse and neglect reporting laws and service delivery systems.

PUBLIC AGENCY RESPONSE

The impetus provided by these events, and the growing public and professional concern for maltreated children stimulated the design and implementation of a wide range of service programs and components. Not only had the problem of child abuse and neglect risen from obscurity, but the legal mandate to provide child protective services to endangered children had mobilized the child welfare community to strengthen, improve, and expand the service delivery system serving abused and neglected children and their families.

Increased identification of abuse and neglect has resulted from efforts to educate the public about their reporting responsibilities, and the availability of hotlines and central registries to accept reports and inquiries. Intervention has improved consequent to the strengthened 24 hour/7 day a week response capacities of CPS (Child Protective Services) agencies. Treatment has been enhanced through the efforts of researchers, practitioners, and agencies working to expand and refine the network of services available to maltreated children and their families. And yet in the midst of this growing rate of reporting and desire to provide treatment services, CPS agencies must protect against overextension of their limited resources. In short, these agencies must learn to comply with their legal mandates in a cost efficient manner, while serving their clients.

Policy:
Child Welfare: An Evolving Legal Bases

ABSTRACT. Child Welfare agencies are today at the crossroads. Facing ever increasing caseloads while threatened by budget reductions, policy makers must rethink the jurisdiction of these agencies so that they can provide necessary services. With the passage of the Federal Adoption and Assistance Child Welfare Act of 1980, it is an opportune time for policy makers, as they take steps to meet this federal Act's compliance requirements, to address this concern. This article discusses some ways in which this can be done by looking at the legal bases by which cases enter the child welfare system, placement is decided, and individual cases are moved through the system.

INTRODUCTION

Today, comprehensive child welfare agencies need a legal base to respond to child welfare cases. The legal bases provides child welfare agencies with authority to intervene in the parent-child relationship, and to exercise coercive authority over parents when necessary, while almost paradoxically, it safeguards the parent's and children's rights when intervention occurs. These laws comprise a mix of Federal legislation, which essentially offers states' guidelines, using federal funds as an incentive; state legislation and regulations; and constitutional precepts, most notably in the area of procedural protections.

FEDERAL LAW

The substantive federal laws concerning child abuse and neglect, foster care, and adoption are found in two acts: *The Federal Child Abuse Prevention and Treatment Act (PL 93-24),* and *The Adoption*

Robert Horowitz is Associate Director, National Legal Resource Center for Child Advocacy and Protection, American Bar Association, 1800 M Street, N.W., Washington, D.C. 20036.

59

and Assistance Child Welfare Act of 1980 (PL 96-272). Additionally, the Indian Child Welfare Act (PL 95-608) addresses Indian
child adoption and custody matters. Together, the Federal Child
Abuse Act and the Adoption Assistance and Child Welfare Act provide a sound shell upon which states may build their child welfare
systems. These two Acts look at child welfare on a continuum rang-
ing from reports of abuse or neglect to the ultimate placement of the
child. In between fall directives concerning such matters as child
protective agency's investigative duties, confidentiality of agency
records, procedural safeguards, preventive services, case plans, and
periodic reviews for children placed out-of-home. While these federal laws are not obligatory on states, certain federal child welfare
funds are available only if a state follows the Acts' provisions.
Given the financial incentives, most states attempt to meet these requirements. Indeed, if a state accepts these federal funds it must
comply with the federal laws and regulations; failure to do so could
result in law suits seeking compliance or even defunding (English,
1981).

STATE LAW: PERMANENCY PLANNING

At the state level, the child welfare system is embodied by legislation, such as child abuse and neglect reporting laws, by agency
regulations, and by state court rules and decisions. At present, given
the emergence of permanency planning as the preeminent social
theory directing child welfare services, state law and regulations are
in transition, as they are striving to facilitate and promote permanence. Some of the legal issues affecting child welfare from three
permanency planning perspectives are: *prioritizing, placement, and
flow* (see Table 1). These issues not only address permanence for
children, but they also respond to growing fears that child welfare
agencies, due to budget cuts at both the federal and state level, are
increasingly unable to assist troubled families. Unfortunately, these
worries are repeatedly being substantiated by the agencies. For example, in a 1982 report to the Maryland legislature, the Maryland
Department of Human Resources predicted serious service deficits
in the coming years. Based upon fiscal year 1982 budget cuts, and
the then anticipated fiscal year 1983 reductions, the Department
foresaw service curtailments to, and even eliminations of 12,500
abused and neglected children and 8,000 foster children.

TABLE 1:   PERMANENCY PLANNING PERSPECTIVES

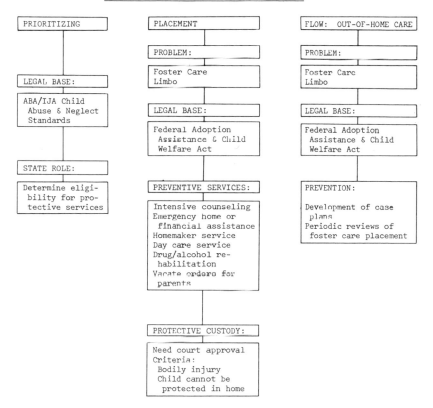

Prioritizing

In the context of child welfare, prioritizing deals with the identification of children and families who should be served by the child welfare system. Assuming that families which voluntarily seek services merit assistance, the problematic area for policy makers concerns involuntary state intervention into the family. In light of alarming statistics such as those cited for Maryland above, on top of what is already recognized as dangerously understaffed child welfare agencies (American Human Association, 1979), the pressure to put a cap on agency caseloads continues to mount. Failure to make intelligent and well considered judgments on which cases to drop from child welfare services, and in turn have these decisions codified, may result in: (a) cases involving serious harm to children going unserved or underserved, (b) agencies intervening inconsistently, (c) perpetuation of foster care "limbo," and/or (d) agencies being sued for injuries sustained by children and families.

At present, statistics suggest that it may be possible to lessen child protective agency caseloads without endangering children. According to the most recent analysis of child abuse and neglect reporting, nearly 60% of all child maltreatment reports to child protective agencies are ultimately deemed unfounded (American Human Association, 1981). The "task" is to look at the "founded" cases and see if they lend themselves to categorization and narrow definition for legislative purposes. While no research to date has done this, over the past several years, there has emerged a body of literature calling for reduced state intervention (Wald, 1976; Goldstein, Solnit, & Freud, 1979), and model acts and standards which offer statutory language toward this end (American Bar Association/Institute of Judicial Administration, 1981; National Advisory Committee for Juvenile Justice and Delinquent Prevention, 1980; Goldstein, Solnit, & Freud, 1979).

These model acts, for the most part, include child maltreatment definitions which are more exacting than the current reporting laws. For example, the American Bar Association/Institute of Judicial Administration (ABA/IJA) child abuse and neglect standards (1981) limit emotional maltreatment to cases evidenced by "severe anxiety, depression, or withdrawal, or untoward aggressive behavior toward self or others." Some commentators go so far as to eliminate entire abuse and neglect categories; for example, unlike the ABA/IJA recommendations, Goldstein, Solnit and Freud (1979) argue for the elimination of emotional neglect, as it defies precise definition and is beyond the state's treatment knowledge. A word of caution is required here: before eliminating entire maltreatment categories it is important to check the requirements of the Federal Child Abuse Act. Some eliminations could make the state ineligible to receive federal child abuse funds.

Another means of legislatively reducing child protective service agency caseloads is to include statutory exceptions to the abuse and neglect definitions. For example, many states specifically exempt from their reporting laws situations arising as a result of the parent's economic condition. Other possible areas of exclusion may include conditions arising from the parent's religious beliefs, life-style, chronic illness, and cultural practices. Such provisions are in tune with those who believe state intervention should be predicated upon both harm to the child and parental fault. However, it should be noted that while the above conditions may preclude an abuse or neglect finding, they should not prevent other state action which may be necessary to save the life of a child, such as a court order of life-saving medical treatment over parental religious objections.

Placement

Few would dispute that state intervention is undesirable if its effects leave the child and family worse off than they previously were. Regrettably, every close study of foster care has supported state intervention critics; children are in out-of-home care indeterminately, experience many, often capricious shifts in residence, and in general are stranded in what has become known as foster care limbo (Children's Defense Fund, 1978; Fanshal & Shinn, 1978). Indeed, this phenomenon led to the enactment of the Federal Adoption Assistance and Child Welfare Act. The Act is an instruction on how to combat such limbo through, among other things, the intervention of case plans and periodic reviews of foster care.

At the state level, numerous steps can be taken by legislators and courts to assure proper placement, which in legal jargon is often referred to as the least restrictive placement, or in the language of the Federal Adoption Assistance Act, the most "family-like setting." These include providing and mandating preventive placement services, toughening substantive and procedural protective custody standards, and continuous monitoring of out-of-home care.

The first two steps may be described as front-end efforts. They also overlap "prioritizing" concerns because they raise the question: what cases merit foster care? When abuse and neglect first comes to a public agency's attention, placement concerns are critical: the guiding principle should be that, whenever possible, placement in the home is preferred. This preference pre-dates permanency planning theory; it rests deeply in our societal values, as attested to by the following declaration from the first White House Conference on Children in 1909:

> Home life is the highest and finest production of civilization. It is the great molding force of mind and character. Children should not be deprived of it except for urgent and compelling reasons.

And in fact, at least by legislative and agency public policy statements, this principle survives today. Yet despite favorable policy, commentators universally criticize agencies trigger finger response to emergency removal of children.

For several reasons there has been an over reliance on protective custody; the most prominent is the agency's desire to "play it safe." Unfortunately, such preemptive behavior is dangerous. Evidence shows that even short separations can have a traumatic psychological effect on parent and child alike (Jenkins & Norman, 1972). Furthermore, once the child is removed from the home the parent-child relationship is further jeopardized: parents may have a hard time visiting children; agencies may unduly restrict parent-child interaction; and services to aid the family, once the child is in a "safe" environment, may be delayed.

PLACEMENT: PREVENTIVE SERVICES

In order to reverse this trend, legislatures must provide child welfare agencies with preventive services which will enable "at risk" families to remain together. Such services may include intensive counseling, emergency home or financial assistance, homemaker services, day care services, and drug/alcohol rehabilitation programs. Admittedly, these services are expensive; however legislators should recognize that the alternative, long-term foster care, is even more costly (Jones, A. J. & Halper, G., 1981), and should explore creative funding mechanisms. The most promising, now enacted in several states, is the creation of a children's trust fund. This fund is typically financed by a $5-$10 addition to the marriage license fee and/or court filing fee for divorces. For example, using this revenue approach, Iowa legislators recently enacted a bill to create a child abuse prevention program within the Department of Social Services. Another possible source of revenue for a children's trust fund was recently considered by the Michigan legislation: this dealt with a proposed amendment to the State tax code allowing taxpayers to designate two dollars of their tax refunds to the trust fund. Congress has also, for the first time, through the Adoption Assistance Act, offered fiscal incentives for states to provide preventive services, reversing a historical trend of higher support levels to foster care over in-home care.

The marshalling of resources for, and monitoring of preventive services today looms critical. Whereas past federal categorical programs, such as Community Mental Health Centers, Alcoholism Treatment and Drug Rehabilitation, and Community Service Programs, could have provided financial assistance for preventive services, the emergence of block grants jeopardizes this usage (Children's Defense Fund, 1982). It is therefore imperative that state legislative bodies commit sufficient block grant funds towards this end. Oversight bodies should be established to assure that child welfare programs receive their share of these revenues. These bodies can take many forms: it may entail a child prevention unit within the social services agency; a legislative oversight committee, akin to the recently created U.S. House of Representatives Select Committee on Children and Youth; or an executive advisory committee. For example, in Washington state the legislature recently created a Governor's Council on Child Abuse and Neglect, funded with $470,000 to contract for community based services (with community agencies required to contribute 25%).

PLACEMENT: PROTECTIVE CUSTODY

Even without a comprehensive prevention program, the child protection agency's practice of removing children should be reexamined. Every state provides by statute for the emergency removal of a child by a police officer, probation officer, and/or child protective service worker if the child is endangered. Typically, the substantive grounds for taking protective custody is the safety, physical and emotional well-being of the child. Taking protective action also requires either pre- or post-removal sanctioning by the court. Like intervention grounds for abuse and neglect generally, substantive grounds for assuming protective custody may require greater specificity.

In fact, most model standards and legislation seek to minimize protective custody. For example, one standard would limit it to preventing threatened *bodily injury* in situations where the *child cannot be protected without removal, i.e.,* in-home services (Juvenile Justice and Delinquency Prevention, 1980). The ABA/IJA (1981) standards provide even more stringent guidelines for emergency removal. Under this standard, emergency removals are authorized only if the remover has "probable cause to believe such custody is necessary to prevent the child's imminent death or serious bodily injury and the parent(s) or other such caretakers is unable or unwilling to protect the child . . ." Recent amendments to the Texas Family Code have incorporated an almost identical standard.

These standards share two critical features: first a significant and identifiable injury to the child must be shown. In these standards, emotional harm, which is harder to demonstrate, was purposely eliminated as grounds for emergency removal. Second, there must be evidence that the child could not be protected in the home.

Both factors are in harmony with the Federal Adoption Assistance Act, which, as the legislative history advises, requires preventive services in every case *prior* to removal unless the "situation in the home presents a substantial and immediate danger to the child which would not be mitigated by the provision of preventive services."

The ABA/IJA standards also provide strenuous procedural protections. Emergency removal is not to occur without prior court approval "unless risk to the child is so imminent that there is no time to secure such court approval." In order to maintain custody, the agency must file a petition with the court no later than the first business day after taking custody; at that time, the court should direct notification to the parents, appoint counsel for the child and refer the petition for prosecution. On the same or next day, a hearing on the emergency temporary custody is to be heard.

In dealing with protective custody requests, courts must avoid summarily rubber stamping agency decisions. Rather, by legislation or court rule, judges should be required to specify conditions which support the removal, as well as conditions of the removal, including parental visitation rights and services which will be available to the child and family. Whenever possible, placement should be with a relative or other appropriate identified person.

Finally, there are times when despite preventive services, the child's health, if left in the care of an abusive parent, may be endangered. Even here, however, there may be recourses short of the child's removal. As a spin off of civil protection orders first introduced in domestic violence cases, states are beginning to consider utilization of vacate orders in child abuse and neglect cases. Under this, an abusive parent may be ordered to vacate the home, thereby permitting the child to remain at home with a supportive parent. For example, recent Iowa legislation extends to the Juvenile Court authority to order an alleged child sexual offender out of the home, "upon a showing that probable cause exists to believe that the sexual offense has occurred and that the presence of the alleged sexual offender is in the child's residence and presents a danger to the child's life or physical, emotional, or mental health.''

FLOW: OUT-OF-HOME CARE

In the child welfare system, ''flow'' may be viewed as what happens to the child and family between the initial intervention by the state and the final case resolution. Legislatively and judicially, steps may be taken to assure smoother passage of individual cases. For purposes of this discussion, flow aspects which arise only after a child has been placed out-of-home will be addressed; this starting point has been picked because flow becomes more critical once a child is removed.

Again the Adoption and Assistance Child Welfare Act promotes the flow of these cases that are designed to avoid foster care limbo. This is accomplished by two means: (a) the development of case plans, (b) periodic reviews of foster care placements. The latter entails two stages of review: periodic reviews of the case plan every six months, and a dispositional review no later than 18 months after the child was placed in care. Many states are presently experimenting with setting up forums to conduct these reviews: for periodic reviews these range from internal agency reviews, citizens foster care review boards, administrative hearings and formal court procedures; for the 18 month dispositional hearing, the options cover review by judicially sanctioned administrative bodies or the courts. Whatever forum settled upon by a state, several procedural safeguards should be afforded the parties. These procedures, at a minimum, would include notice to parents and child's guardian *ad litem* of the scheduled hearing and an opportunity for them to present their viewpoint.

Procedural safeguards notwithstanding, reviews will be to little avail if the judge (or other reviewer) is unwilling to probe agency actions and recommendations or bring cases to a close. In short, judicial training must stress the need for a truly independent review of the case status, beginning with the paramount question: is there a continued need for placement outside the home? Only after this is answered can case plan modifications, if any, be addressed. With the advent of written, signed case plans, judges should feel at ease in assessing progress and the level of agency and parental efforts. In many respects, these plans resemble a contract; setting forth duties and obligations on both the agency's and parent's part, and like a contract are subject to review by a court for compliance and breaches.

Furthermore, as in temporary custody matters, the courts must avoid rubber stamping agency recommendations, especially for non-substantive reasons such as the agency's being understaffed or financially unable to provide needed or necessary services. As a judicial desk book on case reviews properly points out, "if the social service agency feels financially drained by the judicial order, it must seek further appropriations from the legislature. This is the proper way to address financial concerns rather than for the agency to apply pressure on the court to eliminate necessary services" (National Council of Juvenile Family Court Judges, 1980).

Finally, courts must be willing to bring cases to a close. A repeated criticism by social workers of the courts is that judges are overly reluctant to terminate parental rights. Judges must bone up to the fact that at a certain time, after extensive services have been provided to the family, seemingly to little avail, it is appropriate to terminate parental rights, or provide for some other permanent legal remedy such as long-term foster care or legal guardianship. Conversely, judges must also avoid "playing it safe" if the return of the child home is appropriate. Under either scenario, final action is required. Indeed, this need for finality has spurred many commentators to recommend "maximum and minimum time frames allowable at each step of the placement process" (New Jersey Foster Case Assessment Task Force, 1982). For example, the ABA/IJA standards (1982) peg several grounds for terminating parental rights upon time events, such as a child under the age of three having been in placement for two or more years.

CONCLUSION

As states move to institutionalize permanency planning, the legal bases for state child welfare systems must be thoroughly scrutinized. The range of possible reforms is great, far exceeding the few suggestions offered in this article. Yet whatever the reform contemplated, its utility can be analyzed be seeing whether it fits in one or more of the above pigeonholes; prioritization, placement, and/or case flow. Furthermore, once the reform is implemented, it must be installed system wide; a legislative mandate to a child welfare agency may be inoperable if the court, through its own rules, is at odds.

REFERENCES

American Bar Association/Institute for Judicial Administration Juvenile Justice Standards Project. *Standards relating to abuse and neglect.* Cambridge, MA: Ballinger Publishing Co., 1981.

Children's Defense Fund. *A children's defense budget: An analysis of the president's budget and children.* Washington, D.C.: Children's Defense Fund, 1982.

Children's Defense Fund. *Children without homes: An examination of public responsibility to children in out-of-home care.* Washington, D.C.: Children's Defense Fund, 1980.

English, A. Litigation under the adoption assistance and child welfare act of 1980: Insuring availability of services and enforcement of planning mandates for foster children. In H. Davidson, R. Horowitz, M. Hardin (Eds.), *Protecting Children through the legal system.* Washington, D.C.: The American Bar Association, 1981.

Fanshel, D., & Shinn, E. *Children in foster care: A longitudinal investigation.* New York: Columbia University Press, 1978.

Goldstein, J., Freud, A. & Solnit, A. *Before the best interests of the child.* New York: The Free Press, 1979.

Jenkins, S., & Norman, E. *Filial deprivation and foster care.* New York: Columbia University Press, 1972.

Jones, A.J., & Halper, G. *Serving families at risk of dissolution: Public preventive services in New York City.* New York: Child Welfare League of America, 1981.

National Advisory Committee for Juvenile Justice and Delinquency Prevention. *Standards for the administration of Juvenile Justice.* Washington, D.C.: U.S. Department of Justice, 1980.

Wald, M. Intervention on behalf of neglected children: A search for realistic standards. *Stanford Law Review, 1975, 27,* 985.

National Council of Juvenile and Family Court Judges. *Judicial review of children in placement deskbook.* Reno, NV: National Council of Juvenile and Family Court Judges, 1980.

New Jersey Foster Care Assessment Task Force. *A time for reflection, a time for change: Foster care final report.* Trenton, NJ: Division of Youth and Family Services, 1982.

The American Human Association Child Protection Division. *Annual report, 1980 national analysis of official child abuse and neglect reporting.* Denver, CO: The American Humane Association, 1981.

The American Humane Association Child Protection Division. *Child protective services entering the 1980's.* Englewood, CO: The American Humane Association, 1981.

Practice:
Models for Implementing
Child Abuse and Neglect Legislation

Joanne Selinske, MS

ABSTRACT. The problem of child abuse and neglect has been placed on the agenda of social concerns during the last two decades. As a result of heightened awareness of child maltreatment, each state and territory passed legislation mandating the reporting of suspected cases. These laws also provide for the provision of child protective services by public agencies to endangered children and their families. Two state initiatives are described which illustrate the type of program components which have been designed to assist the identification, treatment and prevention of abuse and neglect.

Two states have been selected to illustrate the type of initiatives presently underway to bring the service delivery system into compliance with the reporting legislation. These illustrations have been chosen because they represent cost efficient means of fulfilling parts of the CPS agency mandate—tracking and investigation.

VIRGINIA'S CENTRAL REGISTRY

Legislative Authority

In 1975, the Virginia legislature enacted the Child Abuse and Neglect Law (Va. Code §63.1-248). The Law authorized the Virginia Department of Welfare to establish child protective services within each locale and created a state level child protective services unit. The law delegated a variety of powers and duties to this unit, in-

The author acknowledges the assistance of the Virginia Department of Social Services, and the Illinois Department of Children and Family Services in the collection of information for preparation of this article.

cluding the maintenance of a Central State Registry of all reports of child abuse and neglect within the state.

The 1975 mandate to establish a state central registry was met with strong resistance throughout Virginia. This response was not restricted to the Commonwealth. Consumers nationwide shared concern for the confidentiality of client information and infringement of civil liberties. Many, prompted by a fear of the unknown and reservations about the potential benefits, were hesitant to embrace the implementation of systems which were difficult and cumbersome to implement.

The early widespread skepticism which greeted the Virginia central registry has been largely overcome. Although the use of the Virginia central registry is still criticized by some public and private agencies but opinions have shifted. Many agree that the indexing of cases is essential to the organized functioning of this large service agency. Supporters of the Central Registry now concur that the computerized system provides the most effective means for monitoring the agency's cases.

Operational Benefits for the Central Registry

Besharov (1977-1978), in his discussion of the benefits and failings of central registers, noted that when properly designed and adequately operated, these systems can be a prime tool for the immediate and long-term improvement of child protective systems. Consequent to the investment made in the design and operation of the Virginia system, that State's Central Registry assumes an important role in the overall operation of the child protective services program.

During the period June 1981-June 1982, Virginia received 39,685 reports of suspected abuse and neglect.[1] Virginia law specifies that investigations must be conducted for each of these reports and requires that caseworkers make a preliminary determination of the report within 14 days of its receipt. The automated index of cases handled by the agency provides investigators with information that can aid their diagnosis and evaluation of reports. Data available from the central registry aids caseworkers not only in determining whether abuse and neglect has occurred, but in assessing the risk of future harm to the child. For example, annually 12% of all Virginia

---

[1]Figures provided by the Unit of Child Protective Services, Bureau of Child Welfare Services, Virginia Department of Social Services.

reports, which are assessed as "founded"[2] involve cases in which child protective service staff previously determined that abuse and/or neglect had occurred. Information about previous reports and their outcome can be important to staff who must evaluate the seriousness of a particular situation and determine whether the child's removal from the home or other emergency response is warranted.

The Virginia central registry also performs program monitoring functions. As an example, the central register provides data to administrators identifying cases which have not had dispositions completed with the mandated time frames. Detection of "exception reports," that is, reports not completed within designated time frames, provides program managers with data needed to identify problem areas, a prerequisite to insuring that all staff comply with provisions of the law.

Virginia policy makers have utilized the central registry in identifying random samplings of cases to conduct semiannual reviews of agency performance. In the past, the findings of these reviews have been utilized as the basis of policy decisions addressing, for example, the in-service training needs of caseworkers. The agency has also relied heavily on the central registry to carry out its mandate to prepare an annual report for the Governor and Department Commissioner. Statistical data available from the central registry also has been invaluable to public and voluntary groups throughout the state in assessing the needs of the communities for new or revised service components. Planners, able to identify a significant population of previously underserved clients, have been able to make informed decisions about how to best utilize limited resources. Finally, agency personnel, responsible for encouraging the reporting of suspected maltreatment, can design their public and professional education campaigns based on precise, factual information that is available from the registry.

Challenge for the Future

Virginia's success in establishing a viable, workable central registry in the least seven years, testifies to the dedication of those who believed that it is a vital link in the agency's child protective program. Yesterday's challenge to design central registries which did

---

[2]Reports are judged to be "founded" when agency staff have accumulated "clear and convincing" evidence that abuse or neglect has occurred.

not cave in under an avalanche of reports and paperwork, has been replaced by the challenge to capitalize on these systems proven benefits. Today, policymakers are trying to find ways to further increase the diagnostic, monitoring and research functions performed by the central registry. In Virginia, for example, this means examining and possibly modifying agency policy which mandates that "unfounded" and "unfounded with reason to suspect" reports be immediately purged from the agency records precluding a more careful examination of these categories and types of reports or the way that they were handled by staff. It also requires that staffing patterns be maintained at a level that allows for in-depth analysis of available data in order to meet the increasing demand for information to aid planning and policy making. Given the present economic forecast for human services, Virginia administrators who have enjoyed the benefits of an effective central registry, face the challenge of finding ways to expand the use of a valuable resource while resources supporting publicly funded human service programs diminish.

ILLINOIS

Legislative Authority

In Illinois, the Department of Children and Family Services (DCFS) is the state agency designated to provide child welfare services, including child protective services. The Abused and Neglected Child Reporting Act as amended (1981), expanded DCFS's responsibilities while providing a more detailed set of legislative mandates that govern the investigation and treatment of child abuse and neglect.

Implementation of the Act resulted in a number of significant improvements in the state's child protective service delivery system. This included the creation of a single statewide toll-free hotline for receiving reports of suspected maltreatment, and a computerized data base and tracking system; designation of DCFS as the sole agency responsible for receiving and investigating reports; creation of specialized CPS units to investigate and/or provide or arrange for protective services; authorization for investigative staff to take children into protective custody for up to 48 hours to assure their safety and well-being; and requisition that investigations are initiated within 24 hours of report receipt, and that all investigations are complete within 90 days of report receipt (Illinois, 1982).

In order to carry out the mandates of the Abused and Neglected Child Reporting Act, the Department restructured its service delivery system. This restructuring resulted in the creation of 350 positions within CPS units throughout the state, and the development of comprehensive in-service training for CPS staff to enhance the agency's ability to conduct investigations. The Department also expanded the functions and personnel of the State Central Register, and instituted a computerized information tracking system in order to strengthen the agency's capacity to receive and respond to reports 24 hours a day/7 days a week. In addition, the Department strengthened its emergency response capabilities by assigning investigative staff around the clock, negotiating service contracts with emergency homemakers and foster care facilities, and establishing several emergency shelters (Illinois, 1982).

In early 1981, the Department initiated a series of internal audits to assess the effectiveness of the initiatives that had resulted from changes in the state's reporting act. These reviews identified a number of deficiencies including inadequate documentation of evidence and findings, incomplete investigations, lack of cooperation or consultation with external agencies, and failure to meet established time frames. Analysis of the audit's findings suggested that the staff's focus on family dynamics rather than on the victim/child, contributed significantly to the majority of the deficiencies (Illinois, 1982). The Department subsequently sought to rectify these shortcomings by separating the investigative and service delivery functions performed by staff. In May 1981, Department executives established the Division of Child Protection (DCP). This organizational change was made to support the increased emphasis on the investigative process and to facilitate staff's conduct of accurate, thorough, and timely investigations.

Benefits of Shifting the Focus of Investigations

To insure that the best interests of the child are served, the Department adopted a specific philosophy regarding the protection of children. The new approach directs attention to the child, rather than to the family, as the focal point of the child protective investigation. To accomplish this, the investigation process is narrowly defined for agency staff as a fact finding mission and not a service delivery program. DCP investigative staff do not provide or arrange for ongoing services except when emergency services (e.g., medical treatment, foster care) are needed to protect the child. The purposes of the fact finding process are: to assure the safety and well-being of children suspected to be abused and/or neglected; to determine the validity of reported allegations; to obtain sufficient information to suport Department decisions in court (when necessary); and to give service delivery staff adequate information on "indicated"[3] reports to determine if services are appropriate or necessary to ameliorate family dysfunction (Illinois, 1982).

This reorientation to child protective investigations is applauded by its supporters, for its role in improving and streamlining the investigation process. Advocates for this approach point to the fact that close to 60% of the more than 37,000 reports received annually by the Department are subsequently "unfounded" (unsubstantiated) by DCP investigators, and note that in at least some of these cases the only crisis experienced by the family is the one created by the investigation.

Illinois statute mandates that all child abuse and neglect investigations be completed within 90 days. The Department has established a more stringent goal—the completion of 70% of investigations within 10 days. To accomplish this goal, the Department developed a priority system for response. Reports are assigned one of three priority ratings. These ratings are based on several factors, including the type and severity of the alleged injury, previous history of maltreatment, and the need for court involvement. Investigators perform investigations of varying intensities corresponding to the report's priority. In sum, the priority of a report affects the methodology and minimal number of persons who must be viewed by the investigator, the involvement of external organizations, and the timing and nature of the investigative and/or emergency response.

Concurrent with the organizational and operational changes instituted by the Department, agency administrators decided to prepare an investigative decisions handbook. The development of a handbook to provide staff with practical guidelines for conducting investigations, gathering evidence, making decisions and recording information was seen as the logical next step in strengthening the

---

[3]"Indicated" reports are those in which credible evidence exists that abuse and/or neglect occurred.

agency's intervention capacity.* As a preliminary to writing the handbook, project staff interviewed more than two hundred DCFS staff and community representatives, including judges, state's attorneys, law enforcement officials, medical and social work professionals.

A final component of the initiative undertaken by Illinois to upgrade the quality of service delivery was the design and conduct of in-service training for the agency's child protective investigative staff. This action recognized that development or distribution of sound guidelines for performance would be insufficient to insure that the methods of providing service would improve. In response, the Department began preparation for statewide training of all investigative staff. Training of more than 250 staff was completed in August 1982.

Challenge for the Future

The Illinois Department of Children and Family Services has succeeded in reorienting its approach to the conduct of child protective investigations. Within a short period of time, significant policy, organizational and operational changes have been made in order to redirect the focus of the agency's investigatory functions. Those who will attempt to measure the success of these changes, in assuring that the best interests of the child are served, will not be able to do so without examining the agency's ability to eliminate potential gaps that might surface between its investigative arm and its service delivery program. The child, who has been protected from additional physical harm by being removed to safety by an investigator, will require the attention and sound planning of a service system that is responsive to his permanency planning needs. In order to minimize the harm incurred by the unnecessarily prolonged separation of these children from their natural homes, and to avoid losing children within the foster care system, commitment and careful planning of all child welfare/child protective agencies is required. Illinois' initiative is a significant step towards system reform that is needed to insure the well-being of children.

---

*DCFS staff submitted a proposal to the National Center on Child Abuse and Neglect and secured federal funds to support the development of the handbook. DCFS subsequently contracted with the American Bar Association's National Legal Resource Center for Child Advocacy and Protection and with Data Management Associates, Inc., of New York.

SUMMARY

The initiatives undertaken by the Virginia Department of Social Services (formerly the Department of Welfare), and the Illinois Department of Children and Family Services are examples of the efforts of public agencies to comply with the mandates of child abuse and neglect reporting legislation. Over the past decade, agencies providing child protective service have worked vigorously to keep pace with legislative reforms. In the last ten years alone, we have witnessed significant programmatic improvements in the delivery of services to abused and neglected children and their families. These changes have resulted because of the continued dedication, and in many cases, endurance of administrators, practitioners, researchers, and program planners. The challenge, which they have embraced, remains as the number of children reported to CPS agencies continues to climb, a challenge which will become more difficult to meet as budget cuts decrease the resources available to provide services as well as to stimulate program and system innovations.

REFERENCES

Besharov, D. J. The legal aspects of reporting known and suspected child abuse and neglect. *Villanova Law Review*, 1977-1978, 23(3), 458-520.

Illinois Department of Children and Family Services. *Child abuse and neglect investigation decisions handbook.* Springfield, IL: Illinois Department of Children and Family Services, 1982.

Kadushin, A. Child welfare services (3rd Ed.). New York: Macmillan Publishing Co., Inc. 1980.

The American Humane Association Child Protection Division. Annual report, 1980 national analysis of official child abuse and neglect reporting. Denver, CO: The American Humane Association, 1981. The American Humane Association, in addition to providing annual statistical data on child abuse and neglect, provides training and technical assistance to child protective service agencies throughout the United States and Canada.

CHILD ADVOCACY

Introduction

G. Ness Matthew Gabay, JD

INTRODUCTION

Ever since the U.S. Supreme Court dealt a severe, perhaps mortal, wound to *parents patriae* in the *Gault* decision[1], there has been an increasing number of attorneys involved in the juvenile court system. In many states, attorneys appear not only during the adjudication of allegedly delinquent children, but also for matters involving status offenses, neglect, abuse, dependency, and even emancipation.

The need for this infusion of lawyers—or at least the need for some modification of the system—was well established. All states had adopted a *parens patriae* legal system for children in which the state ostensibly acted to provide care and guidance in the place of the natural parent. Because the state was not considered an adversary of the child, the child was not provided with most "due process" rights accorded an adult. Most states had neglected, however, even in good economic times, to provide the resources necessary to act satisfactorily as a parent. Few objective observers could disagree with the Supreme Court when it wrote in *Kent v. U.S.*:

G. Ness Matthew Gabay is an attorney in The Dalles, Oregon. He was formerly Director of Juvenile Justice Advocacy for the Oregon Council on Crime and Delinquency. Mailing address: 521 E. 7th Street, The Dalles, Oregon 97058.

79

> (T)here may be grounds for concern that the child receives the worst of both worlds: that he gets neither the protections accorded to adults nor the solicitous care and regenerative treatment postulated for children.[2]

Yet the influx of attorneys into the juvenile court system has not uniformly resulted in the improvements for children which the Court might have envisioned when it wrote *Gault* and *Kent*. Indeed, many child care professionals,[3] assert that lawyers have merely obstructed the juvenile courts by placing the "legal interests" of the child above the supposedly "best interests" of the child.

This disappointing turn of events may be the result of three factors: 1) many lawyers are unfamiliar with both legal and social aspects of the juvenile court because law schools do not emphasize juvenile law, 2) lawyers and child care workers do not cooperate adequately because they lack an understanding of the very different perspectives, roles, and ethical considerations of the other profession, and 3) lacking cooperation, the two professions have failed to perceive and further the *real* interests of the child. Thus, historical failings of the system, such as dysfunctional placements, remain uncorrected despite the efforts of the high court.

REFERENCES

1. *In re Gault*, 387 U.S. 1, 87 S Ct 1428, 18 L. Ed. 2d 527 (1967). *Gault* held that restrictions on the liberty of the child decreed by the juvenile court merited "due process" protections against abuse, including the right to be represented by counsel. The court appeared to be influenced by the extensively penal, as opposed to parental, actions of the lower court in the case.

2. *Kent v. U.S.*, 383 U.S. 541, 86 S Ct 1045, 16 L. Ed. 2d 84 (1966), quoted at 383 U.S. 566.

3. The child care profession, as used in this article, is intended to include all persons whose work with children is related to or results from juvenile court action. Within this general grouping there may be subprofessions which may not fully understand or cooperate with each other.

Neither Adversaries nor Co-Conspirators: Creating a Dialogue Between Attorneys and Child Care Professionals

G. Ness Matthew Gabay, JD

ABSTRACT. Lawyers are a relatively new—and permanent—fixture in the juvenile courts. But law school has not well prepared them for the new setting. Lawyers need the aid of child care workers to understand the juvenile court as a social service delivery system. But many child care workers view the lawyers' presence as merely an obstruction in the path which leads to needed treatment for the child.

Both professions must learn to understand the differing perspectives, ethics, and institutional roles of the other. Once this is accomplished, it will be seen that there is no essential contradiction between the "legal interests" and the "best interests" of the child. With an on-going dialogue, both professions can work together to secure the *real* interests of children.

This paper will attempt to explain the differing professional perspectives, demonstrate the desirability of cooperation to further the real interests of the child, and suggest ways to establish an on-going dialogue between the professions.

INADEQUATE TRAINING FOR JUVENILE COURT LAWYERS

Juvenile law has not been a subject of traditional interest in law school. It is not considered one of the "core" subjects (such as contracts, torts, criminal law, or real property), nor is it found on the bar admission tests which qualify graduates to practice law. Those who take the subject, assuming their law school in fact teaches juvenile law, likely will have a choice of only one course, which concentrates, as do most other law courses, on the *law;* that is, the course details the procedure and the substantive rules concerning juveniles. The approach will be adversarial and traditional. With rare exceptions, law schools do not teach the sociology of the juvenile law, do not delve into theories of behavior, do not investigate delinquency as a class-phenomenon or a societal reaction.

Juvenile law courses also tend to ignore the social service aspect of the court. For instance, few attorneys are informed as to the wide variety of alternatives which might be available to juvenile incarceration either prior to, or subsequent to adjudication. Nor are they often aware of the intake considerations applicable to any of these alternatives. In short, juvenile law is taught much as is criminal law; hence the new (and often the experienced) attorney is likely to treat the juvenile case as she/he would the criminal case, even though the two court systems are quite different.

Thus one hears judicial comments that the juvenile court bar is usually well-prepared during the actual adjudication of a child (analogous to a trial), but falters consistently in the pre- and post-adjudication phases. For example, an observer frequently will see an attorney arguing against a court-counselor's recommendation of secure detention for a child; the argument invariably requests that the court return the child to the family, even where it appears that the family may be a major part of the problem. In essence, the attorney requests the judge to do nothing, to retain the status quo. This is analogous to asking the criminal court judge to grant probation, a tactic which is often successful. But in juvenile court, the difference is the judge *is* going to do something. Success in juvenile court means being able to influence what action the judge takes, not in convincing the judge to regrain from acting. Unfortunately, no one has ever pointed this out to many lawyers who practice in juvenile court.

TREATMENT VS. LIBERTY—
A DIFFERENCE IN PERSPECTIVE

The juvenile court system prior to *Gault* was largely considered a medium for providing social services to children. Child care workers tend to concentrate on meeting the perceived needs of a particular child. If, as often is the case, the child resists proffered services, the child care worker seeks to have the court coerce the child into accepting the needed treatment. When the child care worker perceives a need for treatment but the legal justification for court intervention is not present, or cannot be demonstrated with correct procedure, the worker often expresses frustration by claiming the attorney has put the "legal interest" over the "best interests" of the child.

The attorney, on the other hand, begins with the premise that the child is, legally at least, an autonomous being, and for the government to coerce the child into cooperating with any plan—be it termed treatment or punishment—there must be a sufficient legal basis, a justification for government intervention. Equally important, that justification must be demonstrated in accordance with certain accepted legal procedures. These procedures, simply put, are designed to insure fundamental fairness and a rough equity between the power of the state and the vulnerability of the individual.

The institutional role of the attorney is to put the government to the test of demonstrating an adequate legal basis, with adequate legal procedures, for depriving the child of freedom, or the ability to make certain personal decisions. Professional ethics require the attorney to represent the child zealously, and to raise any reasonable defense available to government jurisdiction, unless the child knowingly and voluntarily refuses to raise such defenses. If the legal basis for court jurisdiction is not sufficient, the child care worker must seek other means to get needed treatment to the child. This might result in frustration in a particular case, but operates to protect the entire society agains undue government encroachment.

DYSFUNCTIONAL PLACEMENT
AND THE NEED FOR COOPERATION

Even where the substance and procedure of the law is sufficient for the court to obtain jurisdiction over the child, one must be wary of the placement. Once the child has been diagnosed as "malfunctioning," the natural inclination of the court is to do something to cure the malfunction. But society appears increasingly reluctant to allocate sufficient financial resources for appropriate treatment of children. Thus, rather than creating a treatment program tailored to the specific needs of the child, or perhaps even to the needs of a class of children, the tendency is to place the child in a program which already exists, whether or not it is specific to the needs of the child; *any* program in some states, if only it has an opening. With unfortunate frequency, children are placed in facilities which are dysfunctional for those particular children, and their problems are exacerbated. The court is following its inclination to take action, but the action is inappropriate. Frequent examples include placing victims of sexual or physical abuse in detention centers or even adult jails "for their own protection," and placing runaways alongside robbers and rapists in the state training school. Other examples are more subtle, such as serial placements of dependent children.

Few child care workers would assert such placements positively affect the children involved. The child care worker can help to avoid dysfunctional placements by providing the attorney with a better understanding of the child's psychological predicament, and a knowledge of appropriate placements available or conceptually possible which the attorney may seek to implement.

A phenomenon related to the dysfunctional placement is the practice of "upping the stakes." It appears that once a child has been placed in treatment, it is almost impossible for the system to declare its treatment a failure, and merely release the child. Instead, if a placement fails, frequently "treatment" is escalated to the next level of severity. Thus treatment may get very intense, although neither the original situation of the child nor any subsequent actions by the child considered separately would have warranted such severity. A prime example of this phenomenon arose in my own practice some years back when a diminutive boy of twelve years had been effectively deserted by his parents. He was living with his aged grandmother and exhibiting certain unpleasing behavior: resistive at school, smoking, staying out beyond curfew. The court decided he was beyond the control of his grandmother, and placed him in what appeared to be a good foster home. There he continued to act out in a way that, while not seriously criminal, brought him to the repeated attention of the court. Eventually, he shoplifted two candy bars, and the court sent him to the state training school where he would associate with murderers, burglars and a variety of other offenders. The child care worker in this case opposed that placement. Few child care workers would be likely to see it in the "best interests" of the child. By working closely with the legal profession, they can hope to avoid "upping the stakes" to the point where the child is harmed rather than helped.

OVERCOMING BARRIERS TO COOPERATION

Cooperation between attorneys and child care professionals may be the means to bring a new felicity to the juvenile system, but there are a number of barriers which must be overcome before cooperation can be achieved.

A first step towards increased cooperation between the two professions might well be to reevaluate whether "legal interests" and "best interests" really are contradictory. If "best interests" means providing the child with an environment in which the child can grow, in which the child has a sense of caring and concern, and in which the child can learn socially acceptable ways of relating to others, then it appears that careful consideration of a proposed environment and an institutionally fair process for determining whether the child will be placed in that environment are essential. "Legal interests" represent no more than that. Indeed, the child's perception of the fairness of his/her situation may be determinative of the success of the treatment plan, assuming a functional placement was selected in the first place.

Perhaps a greater barrier to cooperation between the professions is the simple lack of contact that exists between them. When I gave a seminar on cooperation to an international group of child care workers in Canada,[1] I discovered that most of the participants believed attorneys obstruct the provision of services to children, but few had any contact with attorneys in their professional lives, and only juvenile court workers had regular contact of any sort with lawyers.

Frequent contact should be the norm. From the lawyer's position, contact with the juvenile court counselor and with treatment workers and psychologists where appropriate should be made as routine as the defense attorney's request for discovery from the prosecuting attorney. It should be on the checklist for every juvenile case. But what if, as usual, it is not? Child care workers whether in the juvenile court or in treatment would do their clients an important service by establishing contact with the child's attorney. It would be appropriate to brief the attorney on the child's history, assessed needs, and resources available to meet those needs, in so far as professional ethics allow. By interpreting psychological tests, discussing various options, and looking to find a way to provide the most appropriate treatment in the least restrictive setting, the child care worker may be able to combine with the attorney to achieve the most appropriate court decisions.

In a general setting, professional contact may be promoted by professional associations. The state association of child care workers (CCWA) can be an important resource for the bar association. The CCWA can help educate lawyers on the social service aspects of the juvenile court, on the basic psychological concepts of the court, on alternatives to detention, and on treatment opportunities available in the state. By reaching out to the bar as a professional body, child care workers can enhance their own effectiveness.

A third barrier to cooperation may be the professional ethics of each body. Child care workers are in somewhat of a bind in this regard, in that traditional ethics of confidentiality may keep them from discussing a client with the client's lawyer, yet if called upon, they may have no privilege to prevent testimony as to the child's statements made to them.

One approach to this problem is to recognize that the attorney is required to keep confidential all information received from or about a client, unless the client expressly authorizes disclosure (with minor exceptions not relevant here). This is not only a privilege preventing the attorney from testifying in court, but applies as a prohibition against the attorney revealing to anyone information gained about the client without the client's permission. With this understanding, a child care worker *may* be ethically freed to discuss the child with the child's attorney, insofar as ethics would allow the worker to discuss the case with the child him/herself. The attorney who possesses information about the child which the child care worker does not, and which would be helpful in formulating a treatment plan, may request permission of the child to divulge the information to the worker. However, the child care worker must realize that the child's attorney is not likely to reveal information which the juvenile court could properly require the child care worker to reveal in court.

A fourth barrier to cooperation may be the impression the attorney gives others. As mentioned above, attorneys are trained as advocates and many tend to think as adversaries. But also being professionals, few attorneys let their adversarial posture degenerate into personality. Thus the approach to an attorney, as perhaps to all persons, is very important. If the child care worker understands the professional posture of the attorney and conveys the impression that she/he is concerned for the child, and wishes to help the attorney represent the child more fully, the attorney is likely to be quite receptive to professional overtures. It may be that with the broader perspective a lawyer gains of the child's situation, the lawyer might use his/her considerable influence with the child and family to gain some objectives the court never would have been able successfully to enforce.

ESTABLISHING A DIALOGUE

Improved interaction between attorneys and child care professionals is not likely to occur spontaneously. A dialogue between the professions must be created. What follows is a strategy for establishing such a dialogue. The force to implement these suggestions might be provided by child care associations, bar associations or bar committees on juvenile law, law school administrators, legislators, individual attorneys and child care workers, or any individual or organization with energy and a civic inclination.

Law schools must begin to place a greater emphasis on juvenile law generally, and particularly on the non-legal or social service aspects of the juvenile court. They must attempt to educate law students not only on the law, but on how to be competent practitioners of the law. To this end, law schools might include child care professionals as guest lecturers in juvenile law, might provide credit for taking university courses in subjects such as the sociology of juvenile delinquency, and might seek to provide clinic credits for internships with local juvenile departments.

Schools of social work must increasingly include attorneys and legal issues in their curricula, particularly in courses which deal with juveniles. Actions similar to those suggested for law schools might be appropriate.

State bar licenses should be limited to fields in which the attorney has demonstrated competence in a state bar exam or by other means.[2] That is, if an attorney wishes to practice juvenile law (or real property, etc.) she/he must demonstrate competence to do so. This might be accomplished by having elective subjects on the bar exam, e.g., if a law student wished to be licensed to practice in juvenile court, the student must elect to answer the bar exam section on juvenile law. This might also be accomplished by establishing a state bar section on juvenile law which an attorney would have to join prior to practicing juvenile law. Joining the section might involve taking an exam or a certain number of Continuing Legal Education courses.

The state bar association should combine with the state child care workers association to produce continuing education materials for both professions that explain the legal and the social service aspects of the juvenile court. This might include articles in professional journals and periodic seminars where attorneys could learn of the treatment/placement alternatives currently available, and child care workers could learn of current legal/legislative developments.

State child care associations must become active politically in search of adequate resources for children. State bar associations should expand their lobbying efforts to include this goal. In addition, laws must be changed to limit the intake of children into facilities that are not designed or operated to treat the child's particular situation. It is time to stop looking to the state training school as a warehouse for children with no place else to go.

Local bar associations should seek to have joint meetings with child care associations to promote interchange of ideas and factual information such as what alternatives are available to secure detention.

Individual attorneys and child care workers must begin to seek each other out in particular cases in order to provide the best service to children. If a worker observes a dysfunctional placement, she/he must try to interest the child's (former) lawyer to seek redress. If a placement is working, even if the child commits further offenses, the child care worker must combine with the lawyer to secure a court decision returning that child to the placement.

Both professions should make the child and the child's family integral members of the decision-making process where possible.

CONCLUSION

There is no essential contradiction between "best interests" and "legal interests"; both merge to form the "real interests" of the child, that is, the securing of a safe, caring growth producing environment without improper or undue intervention in the life of that child. The juvenile court is an active social service system that will take some action regarding a child before it. Both the legal and the child care professions have, or *should* have, the mutual goal of influencing the action of the court so that judicial decisions are legally and developmentally sound for the child.

This set of conclusions implies that there is a need for increased cooperation between the professions. Contact, communication, and cooperation are essential to providing better, more effective services for children. Even so, child care workers and lawyers must recognize that they are two separate professions, not co-conspirators. The differences in perspective discussed above are more than chimeric. There will always be a certain amount of adversarial process in any court proceeding. The key is to establish a dialogue by which an informed, functional, positive choice can be made about a child in juvenile court.

With increased cooperation, the real interests of the child may begin to emerge from both the supposed "legal" and "best" interests, fulfilling a promise articulated by the Supreme Court almost 20 years ago.

REFERENCES

1. "Conference '82—Emerging as a Profession," Banff Springs Hotel, Banff, Alberta, May 2-6, 1982.

2. This issue—specialization in law—is currently one of great controversy in several state bar associations. Whatever the merits of this suggestion, it should not be assumed that it could be implemented with ease.

Practical Techniques for Change

Gwen G. Morgan, MS

ABSTRACT. Policy change requires documentation of a problem, pinpointing the official document, and agreement on a feasible solution. Factors inhibiting communication and consensus are identified. Content-related techniques for change include stakeholder identification, mechanisms for group decision-making and the building of trust, group discipline, and avoidance of jargon. Process-related techniques for change include creating an appropriate structure, networking, gathering and presenting information, and following the legislative process.

Public policy is slow to change. Laws and administrative practices often reflect outmoded concepts about services for children, and may be causing serious harm. Professionals whose assumptions are based on new knowledge are impatient when they find their knowledge not reflected in policy (Mearig, 1978). Unfortunately, they seldom have access to knowledge and theories on affecting the policy process (Lindblom, 1980; Lindblom & Cohen, 1979).

In order to influence policy, the following conditions should be met: First, there must be agreement that there is a problem. The more dramatic the problem, the more likely the change. Policymakers are more likely to flee from perceived evils than to pursue positive goods. Even when positive goods are pursued, there must be a defined problem; for example, a lack of community support for something needed, or a failure of the market to supply it within the price that families can afford to pay. Data on the magnitude of the problem are essential.

Second, the problem must be defined. It is not enough to crusade for change; the change must be precisely identified. In what law, administrative rule, or court decision is it written that the present poli-

---

Gwen G. Morgan is a lecturer at Wheelock College, 35 Pilgrim Road, Boston, Massachusetts 02215.

cy must be followed? What wording is needed, and where, for a new policy to be implemented?

Third, there must be a feasible solution within the cost that the public is willing to bear. Further, there must be widespread agreement among many sectors of the public that there is a problem, and that the solution being proposed is the desirable one. The policy-making process is therefore quite different from policy analysis alone, and involves complex techniques for building the needed agreements across all factions within a specialized field, across professional fields, and with the members of the general public. The policy process is driven by the persuasive packaging of information for the purpose of building that needed consensus about the nature of the problem and the desirable and feasible solution. It depends upon the art of communication among those who differ.

FACTORS INHIBITING COMMUNICATION BETWEEN PROFESSIONALS IN LAW AND HUMAN SERVICES

Lawyers and various human services personnel may have some difficulty in initial communication because their education may have created some different underlying assumptions and concepts, which may get in the way of the common ground they share in working for change (Winograd, 1971).

Concepts of rights. Human service professionals tend to think in terms of human rights. Once knowledge is acquired that something is a basic human need, it is thought of as a right. Lawyers, however, see rights in terms of remedies. A human right is not valuable until some identified person must meet the need and be held accountable for doing so.

Clashing rights. Any right of one person may interfere with the rights of another person. There are no pure rights. The task for any society is to arrive at the desired trade-offs to decide how much to impede the freedom of some individuals in order to guarantee the rights of other individuals. Human service professionals tend to become confused in the fact of clashing rights because they assume they can guarantee everybody's rights without trade-offs.

Concepts of authority. Both types of professionals are distrustful of the arbitrary use of authority. Lawyers have developed practical approaches to the limitation of authority of the government through due process and various rules for structuring the use of discretion. All of this is often incomprehensible to the human service professional and viewed as red tape. Human service professionals may view police powers as inherently bad, and talk about "flexibility" without defining what they mean.

Perceptions of power. Human services professionals, unfamiliar with policy formulation, are more likely to assume their own powerlessness than lawyers. They may accept laws as givens, while lawyers assume they can be improved. Lawyers, however, may expect a higher degree of irrationality in the legal system, and feel greater satisfactions with smaller improvements than the human service professionals, who may burn out when they do not achieve the ideal at once.

FACTORS INHIBITING AGREEMENT IN THE HUMAN SERVICE FIELDS

Different specializations. There are a number of disciplines within the human services fields, each with its own knowledge base and concepts. Communication may be a Tower of Babel. Individuals may define their own identity to some degree in terms of their specialized field, and may be defensive of its present and future interests. Even though each of us may sincerely believe that the interests of children and families are best served by defending the interests of our specialized perspective, that defense is a different interest not identical with the interest of children. Lack of awareness of the differences characterizes these idealistic specializations.

Domain overlap. There is a good deal of overlap of interest of the different professional disciplines, and in the agencies of government to which they relate. There are further overlaps in government for another reason, its structure. Government is generally organized by functional mission: health, education, transportation, etc. Yet we also create government agencies for particular client groups: welfare families, the aging, children, etc. The interests of any client group cuts across all functional missions, and the functions cut across all client group interest. Client group agencies should be viewed as integrating mechanisms across the functions, but they sometimes take on rival roles to the agencies organized by function. Further, when government creates a decentralized structure, tension exists between the interests of the central agency and those of the regional offices. Finally, there are obvious domain overlaps among different levels of government: federal, state, county, and municipal (Hanf, 1978).

When there is domain overlap, the participants tend to struggle for autonomous control in order to be maximally effective. These struggles can seldom be won since the interests of all participants are legitimate and continuing. Much energy is wasted in the tensions of domain overlap that might more productively be spent in sharing.

Roles perspectives. In addition to different domains of interest, there are also different roles that may have quite different perspectives. The front-line worker in the field, the administrator at the service level, the administrator at the bureaucratic level, and the consumer of the service will have varying views on issues such as unmet needs, wages and working conditions, quality of service, costs and affordability. All these perspectives have validity and are needed, but communication across roles may be very difficult unless individuals can broaden their perspective.

Consensus. Policy is an agreement that government will behave in certain expected ways, and change is accomplished only when there is widespread new agreement that there is a problem and that a proposed solution is the right one. Skills in building consensus are therefore critical.

Consensus is a group decision-making process that is not the same as unanimous agreement, on the one hand, or a majority vote, on the other (Schein, 1969). Unanimous agreement almost never happens. Bringing a matter to a vote, which sounds democratic, tends to be so divisive in many cases that it interferes with policy implementation. Consensus, in contrast to these two methods, means that members of a group are in the end willing to agree to a decision that might not be the top choice of every member, because the process of arriving at the decision permitted time for free expression of opinion and full opportunity to influence the direction of the decision.

Consensus is needed in two major stages of the policy process. First, anyone seeking a change in policy needs to check to see that there is reasonable consensus on the content of the policy among all the key individuals and groups that have a special reason to care about the policy, the major stakeholders. Content discussion and consensus building techniques will be needed along with stakeholder analysis. Second, when the policy change is proposed in the public arena, a wider consensus must be built among legislators, other stakeholders, and the general public, and adaptations in content may continue to be needed, and further work on consensus among stakeholders continued.

TECHNIQUES FOR CHANGE

There are two major ways in which skills are needed. One set of techniques has to do with the content of the policy change, and the building of consensus about it; the other set of techniques addresses the processes of policy change.

Content related techniques. Sometimes the problem to be addressed is so clear, and the solution so obvious that all participants can happily move forward together on the lobbying processes, with little attention paid to details about the content. On the other hand, sometimes a change may be so threatening to existing interests that much work must be spent on building trust among the groups that have a stake in the policy. Otherwise, the result is often a stalemating effect. One group does not have the power to block change. Sometimes a powerful legislator can cut through covert disagreements with strong public support, but that is not always possible. To avoid the stalemating potential, it is important for advocates to be aware that skills may be needed in consensus building among stakeholders.

Identify the stakeholders. All the groups directly affected by the present policy and the future policy will likely have strong feelings about it; they are the major stakeholders. Of course, not all stakeholders may go along with a change because some may have a vested interest in the system as it is; they may become opponents of the policy. The more you can get stakeholder support, the easier it is to send clear messages and build a public consensus. Major stakeholders will include providers of a service, academic experts, consumers, and others.

If there is stakeholder resistance, take time. The best technique for getting people to buy into a change is to create a process they can influence. If someone has strong feelings and an interest in an issue, and cannot affect the process, she/he will become anxious and very distrustful. There should be clearly adequate time for full discussion, even as long as a year in some cases. There should always be a deadline at the end so that the process does not become an endless delay.

Permit review and improvement of the policy as widely as feasi-

ble. Circulate drafts for revision as soon as one can be prepared that appears broadly acceptable; be responsive to concerns that are expressed. Date and label drafts as such; acknowledge the participation of those concerned. The final product should be owned by as many people as possible. If the change is very controversial, try to share credit as widely as possible.

Have open meetings. If the group working on the policy makes it clear that other participants are welcome, other groups will come to the extent that they perceive the importance of the outcome.

Hold regularly scheduled information sharing meetings. Anybody may come to these meetings to hear accurate information about what is being discussed, and offer comments and suggestions. If possible, set up an agenda that always starts with a basic orientation for new participants, goes on to presentation of information, then full discussion. Since no decisions are made and information is shared in two directions, this technique builds trust.

Make sure everyone at a meeting has a basic amount of the same information before discussion. This can be done through briefings and handouts. If groups try to discuss any controversial issue before they have information in common, a high level of anxiety can be generated.

Avoid whenever possible putting a new group in the position of having to make a group decision. New groups can express individual opinion, but are not able to make a group decision until they have been given time to get to know each other, a process that may take longer than the time available. When there is not time for the many individuals to become a group, other techniques work better. One is for someone in advance of the group meeting to get opinions from each participant on a one-to-one basis, either by telephone or interview. Present the data on areas of strong agreement and disagreement to the group. Another technique is individual polling for individual expressions of concern, in writing, and feeding the information back to the group. If a new group needs to make a collective decision, the basic order for discussion that works best is (a) introductions, (b) getting all relevant information presented to the group as fully and efficiently as possible, (c) eliciting individual expressions of opinion and concern as fully as possible without permitting proposals for group decision such as motions, and (d) attempting to reach a group decision through parliamentary procedures. Since most people believe they should begin making decisions at once, this lengthy process will cause frustration and a sense of failure if not presented well. However, it is far less frustrating than trying to get a new group to make decisions.

Reach out to stakeholder groups. Not all those whose interests are affected by a policy change may be participating in the development of a new policy. If they have a major stake in the policy, they should receive information whether or not they participate. Unless they have been fully informed and invited to participate in the policy development, they are left free to oppose the results.

Develop discipline within your own group. During a process of consensus building, it is destructive for members of a group to be expressing differing opinions to legislators. The disagreement should be ironed out within your group, and between your group and other groups. Take someone with you if you visit a legislator, and make a conscious effort not to work at cross-purposes with other groups. Human service professionals have a reputation for being so individualistic and idealistic that they cannot propose a coherent, single policy that a legislator can support safely. That reputation can be used to justify a lack of support for human service issues. It is preferable to work out details among the different factions rather than having each group proposing different solutions to the legislators and other policy-makers. Further, if we are to form stronger alliances and build trust within the human service field, members must behave in a trustworthy manner.

Avoid jargon. When communicating with anyone outside your professional discipline, use common language. Jargon is extremely useful within specialized fields for two reasons. First, it signals very complex meanings in very few words to individuals who have read similar literature and have been educated in the same conceptual framework. It is short-cut language. Further, it signals a value system and is an important trust-building method. When this language is used with those who do not share a common knowledge base, however, it communicates nothing. At best, it may be seriously misunderstood. An example is the word "socialization." This could be (and often is) associated with socialism or even communism. Those within a field of specialization, however, are often unwilling to give up cherished terminology because they want to use it to signal trust. It is important to interpret the need to communicate in common language in order to build a broad base of support across disciplines and with the general public, or else the specialized professionals will insist on the use of words that may arouse public fears that can be manipulated by the opposition.

PROCESS RELATED TECHNIQUES

Once there is a fairly large consensus on the content of a needed policy change, skills are needed in building a broad base of support that includes the less vested stakeholders, policy-makers, and the general public. Change takes place in a number of policy arenas. Advocates will have pinpointed one of the following: Standards that need changing by an administrative process; prior court decisions that need to be changed by lawsuit; structure of government changes that might be accomplished by Executive Order or a Governor, or by law, or else a change that can be made by passage of legislation, or in budget language. In the interest of brevity, the following discussion will focus on the legislative process, primarily, that which includes new bills and the budget. Further, the focus will be primarily on state and federal legislative processes, although some policies are set locally.

Decide on your campaign structure. Some existing organization may take on the tasks, reaching out to and including other individuals and other organizations, if the other organizations are willing to participate in that way. Several existing organizations might form an ad hoc coalition for the purpose of bringing about the needed change (Briggs, 1977). Such a coalition might work together just for the purpose of a particular bill, it might try to become a permanent organization, or it might create a loose working relationship that holds up over time for general working together on a number of bills and the annual budget.

An example of the latter came about naturally when a fairly large number of different advocacy groups happened to rent space in the same building. Their directors and other nearby advocates began sharing information at a regularly held weekly meeting, calling themselves "El Whammo." A sub-group for children, called "El Kiddo," met afterward, and became very effective. The informal coalition dissipated after a fire in the building forced the groups to find other space. The example illustrates the transitory nature of much structure for advocacy. Once the structure disappears, however, the trust relationships remain between the individuals involved, and can be called on in new work relationships.

Sometimes a new organization is created for an advocacy effort. If there is no other organization with a similar mission, creating a new organization is relatively simple and generates enthusiasm. If there is domain overlap with existing organizations, this fact can interfere with the needed trust, and divert energy into time-consuming discussions of organizational structure. Because of this, it is sometimes so difficult to create a new organization or use an existing one for leadership, that new ways for working together are evolving.

Networking (Lipmack & Stamps, 1982) has been described as the creation of ''unorganizations'' with special characteristics of informality, equality of membership, and broad distribution of power in contrast to traditional organizations. Networking may, therefore, be an important organizational strategy (Perrow, 1972). Networking is also an advocacy technique of building on trust relationships that will be used in any case, regardless of the organizational structure, to impact the policy development process (Dluhy, 1980) or the sharing of resources (Sarason, 1977).

There are a number of political action committees for children that have successfully participated in the electoral process to influence the positions of candidates for office on children's issues, and to elect candidates with a concern for children and/or defeat those with poor records. These campaign-like organizations (see Appendix) may or may not stay in existence between elections.

More permanent organizations, such as the California Children's Lobby or the Massachusetts Advocacy Center work on particular issues through lobbying legislation or monitoring bureaucratic action. Whether permanent or transitory, these activities build trust relationships that carry over into other advocacy efforts for years to come.

Package information to support the policy change. Facts are the fuel that drive the policy process (Children's Defense Fund). Data must be gathered that demonstrate that there is a policy problem, the magnitude of the problem, the consequences of failure to act, and the cost of the solution. While it is important to gather as much data as possible, it is equally important to organize facts in a very brief interocular presentation. It hits you between the eyes. The perfect material is a one-page handout that presents the data, pinpoints the needed change, and is attractively laid out with plenty of empty space to relieve print monotony. It should have the name and telephone number of the group that prepared it.

Form alliances and network. There are many groups that may not be aware that they are stakeholders; it will be important to identify them (Biklen, 1974). For example, on the issue of eliminating exemptions to licensing laws for day care centers, advocates may find support from the fire safety lobby that might not even know of the issue. Organized labor might be informed of the effect that a budget issue has on wages. While working for passage of legislation, advocates will involve all the people they involved earlier in the development of the proposed policy and in the gathering of the data, they will identify as many others as possible, and they will reach out to call on the trust relationships their members have formed in previous advocacy efforts.

Use the media to reach the general public. Press releases should include both big city and suburban press. Radio talk shows will cover an issue in depth seldom permitted by the print media. Television news, talk shows, and features help to dramatize an issue. Creative use of these means is important. Legislators respond directly to advocates, but they are also responding to the views of the general public.

Know the timetable for a bill. State and federal legislative processes are different. You can get material on how a bill becomes a law from your state legislator and congressional representative (Congressional Quarterly, 1982). Know this process so that you will be able to respond with the right strategy at each point. Plan your calendar according to the legislative timetable (Dear & Patti, 1981). Since the budget is a bill, and goes through the legislative process each year (Center for Community Change, 1978), this ongoing process will need attention every year. Testimony (Kleinkauf, 1981) must be prepared during the period for public hearings; and letters (U.S. Congress, 1982) directed at different points in the process to appropriate committee members, to legislators for floor discussion, and to the leadership and the Governor.

Visits to legislators. Those closely lobbying a bill should become well acquainted with the legislative staffs, with the leadership, and with members of the committee. Advocates from the legislator's own districts should know their representatives on a personal basis, and visit them. Key, well-informed members of the group should visit the Committee chair and staff, touch bases with the Governor's legislative staff person, and other legislative liaisons from relevant departments of government on the issue.

It is important to go personally to visit legislators. They have a right to expect discipline from advocates. Send just a few people, only take a reasonable amount of time, and represent the views of many. Be friendly, courteous, and as brief as possible. Decide in advance what you want the legislator to do, and speak to a limited agenda without wandering. Take along your one-page handouts to leave with the legislator(s). Another useful device is a "talking paper." On a single page, this is a brief outline that presents a few very basic points that you will cover in your visit. For further elaboration, each point can have its own backup sheet(s) with more factual documentation. This can be given to the legislator for his own personal file. If you are asked a question you cannot answer, send the answer later. Listen carefully to the legislator's questions as clues to their thinking. Try to get a solid answer as a result of your meeting, either at the time of your meeting, or later.

Be there when testimony is heard and when votes are taken. A large number of people should be present when hearings are held, but just a few people can follow a bill. It is important to be present whenever action is taken at committee meetings or on the floor. There needs to be a system, such as a telephone tree, for alerting the network about action being taken. The task is time-consuming, and potentially overwhelming unless the person doing it can call on some reserve people at times. Otherwise, burn-out and overload will certainly occur.

Stay with the legislation. If it does not pass the first year, improve it based on the knowledge gained at hearings and at meetings. File it for a second year, and if necessary, for a third year. Possibly parts of it can pass even if the entire legislation does not. Have a temporary fall-back position, if necessary, that will take you as far as seems politically feasible toward your ultimate objective. When the legislation does pass, follow through with its implementation. You should be assured, even at the same time the bill is introduced, that money for implementation is added to the budget as soon as it appears likely the bill will pass. Prior to passage, you will also want to discuss whether there is adequate staff for implementation, in number, and also whether the right staff is available in terms of competence and values. These questions are administrative, and the scene will shift after passage to the agency designated to administer it, and possibly to the Governor's office.

The policy processes are remarkably responsive to those who work together and can make a good case for the action they propose. The greatest barrier to effective advocacy may be the failure of the human service professionals to perceive this responsiveness and their own power to compel it. Perhaps more effective alliances with the legal professionals will overcome that problem.

REFERENCES

Biklen, D. *Let our children go: An organizing manual for advocates and parents.* Syracuse: Human Policy Press, 1974.

Briggs, J. *The coalition and coalition building.* Washington, D.C.: National Self-Help Resource Center Inc., 2000 S Street, Washington, D. C. 2009, undated.

Center for Community Change. *Citizen involvement in the local budget process.* Washington, D. C.: Center for Community Change, 1978.

Children's Defense Fund. *Where do you look? Whom do you ask? How do you know? Information Resources for child advocates.* Washington, D.C.: Children's Defense Fund, 1978. Other current CDF publications are also helpful.

Congressional Quarterly Inc. *Current American Government.* Washington, D.C.: Congressional Quarterly Inc., Fall 1980. CQ publishes this guide twice annually; the most current issue is likely to be the most useful.

Day Care Council of America. *An advocacy handbook.* Washington, D.C.: Day Care Council of America, September 1981.

Dear. R., & Patti, R. Legislative advocacy: Seven effective tactics. *Social Work,* July 1981, 289-295.

Dluky, M. *Social change: Accessing and influencing the policy development process.* Washington, D.C.: U. S. Department of Health and Human Services, 198.

Hanf, K., & Scharph, F. Interorganizational policy making: Limits to coordination and central control. Beverly Hills, CA: Sage Publications, 1978.

Kleinkauf, C. A guide to giving legislative testimony. *Social Work,* July 1981, 297-303.

Lindblom, C. The policy-making process. Englewood Cliffs, N.J.: Prentice-Hall, 1980.

Lindblom, C., & Cohen, D. *Usable knowledge, social science and social problem solving.* New Haven: Yale University Press, 1979.

Lipnack, J., & Stamps, J. *Networking: First report and directory.* Garden City, N.Y.: Doubleday & Co., 1982.

Marlow, H. *How to affect legislation before it affects you.* Los Angeles, Grantsmanship Center, 1978.

Mearig, J. *Working for children: Ethical issues beyond professional guidelines.* San Francisco: Jossey-Bass, 1978.

Perrow, C. *Complex organizations: A critical essay.* Glenview, Ill.: Scott Forsman, 1972.

Sarason, S., Carrol, C., Matton, K., Cohen, S., & Lorentz, E. *Human Services and resources networks.* San Francisco: Jossey-Bass, 1977.

Schein, E. *Process consultation: Its role in organizational development.* Reading, MA: Addison-Wesley, 1969, p. 52 ff.

U.S. Congress. Tips on writing a member of congress. *U.S. Congress Handbook.* Washington, D.C.: U.S. Congress, 1982.

Winograd, I. *Delivery of services in a regulated society.* Milwaukee: University of Wisconsin, Department of Social Work, 1971.

POLITICAL ACTION COMMITTEES

Operating at the National Level

1.　KidsPac
   William W. Harris, Treasurer
   80 Trowbridge Street
   Cambridge, MA 02138
   617/492-2229

B. Operating Within States

1. Political Action Committee on Behalf of Young Children
   John E. Kyle, Treasurer
   963 W. Cross Street
   Ypsilanti, MI 48197
   313/485-7768 (h) or
   313/485-2000 (w)

2. The Political Action Committee to Protect Children and Youth
   Ronald Foloway
   12 West 37th St., 8th Floor
   New York, NY 10018
   212/564-9220

3. Illinois Advocates for Children
   Tom Fee, Treasurer
   R.R. #2, Box 27
   New Lenox, IL 60451
   -or call-
   Elizabeth Magee 217/546-6243
   Lana Hostetler 217/528-4287

4. The Campaign for Families and Children
   11 Beacon Street, Room 901
   Boston, MA 02108
   617/365-8565

5. Californians for Children
   Ed Warren, Treasurer
   P.O. Box 906
   San Francisco, CA 94101
   -or call-
   Maryann Suggs 714/599-4741

II. Voter Education Projects

Project Vote
1201 Sixteenth St., NW
Suite 233
Washington, D.C. 20036
202/649-5954

Merle Caryl
c/o Clients Council
P.O. Box 342
Eugene, OR 97440

Claude Jackson, Chairman
Sumpter County Citizens for Better Government
P.O. Box 37
General Delivery
Panola, AL 35477

Ms. D. Fields, Director
Cradle Nursery, Inc.
1301 Northwest Sixth Court
Fort Lauderdale, FL 33311

Voter Education Project (11 southern states)
52 Fairly Street, NW
Suite 360
Atlanta, GA 30303
404/522-7495

Southwest Voter Registration Education Project
(5 southwestern states)
201 North Saint Mary's
Suite 501
San Antonio, TX 75205
512/222-1224